MANAGING THE MANAGERS

Managing the Managers

by Edward McSweeney

Introduction by Perrin Stryker

HARPER & ROW, PUBLISHERS

NEW YORK, HAGERSTOWN,

SAN FRANCISCO, LONDON

1817

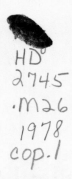

"A Score Card for Rating Management" originally appeared in *Business Week.*

MANAGING THE MANAGERS. Copyright © 1978 by Edward McSweeney. Introduction copyright © 1978 by Perrin Stryker. All rights reserved. Printed in the United States of America. No part of this book may be used or reproduced in any manner whatsoever without written permission except in the case of brief quotations embodied in critical articles and reviews. For information address Harper & Row, Publishers, Inc., 10 East 53rd Street, New York, N.Y. 10022. Published simultaneously in Canada by Fitzhenry & Whiteside Limited, Toronto.

FIRST EDITION

Designed by Eve Callahan

Library of Congress Cataloging in Publication Data

McSweeney, Edward.
    Managing the managers.
    Bibliography: p.
    Includes index.
    1. Directors of corporations—United States.
2. Industrial management—United States. 3. Corporations—United States—Management. I. Title.
HD2745.M26 1978   658.4'2   77–3761
ISBN 0–06–012959–X

78 79 80 81 82 10 9 8 7 6 5 4 3 2 1

Contents

Introduction

by Perrin Stryker

Managers do not take kindly to being managed. And chief executive officers who have gained the top of the management ladder are particularly contemptuous of outsiders who would venture to judge or control their decisions. Ordinarily, they learn early to apply a special treatment that effectively incapacitates those outsiders who are their superiors on boards of directors.

This treatment, normally a private matter confined to board rooms, received an unexpected airing in 1977 when *The New York Times* published an interview with Harold M. Williams shortly after President Carter had nominated him to the chairmanship of the Securities and Exchange Commission. Mr. Williams, who was the head of the business school of the University of California at Los Angeles but had been chairman of a big conglomerate, Norton Simon Inc., recalled: "One of my colleagues used to suggest that the way to handle boards is to treat them like mushrooms. Keep them in the dark, water them well and cover them with horse manure."

The treatment has been intensified in recent years as more and more CEOs have annexed the title of board chairman and thereby doubled their opportunities for withholding information from directors, cultivating their approbation and burying them in trivia and optimistic talk. Small wonder, then, that directors have remained such ridiculously easy targets for economists, congressmen, novelists and cartoonists.

Among other things, directors have been called passive, compliant, somnambulant, the puppets of management, a legal fiction, a necessary but impotent nuisance, and the CEO's back-seat drivers. Generations of cartoonists have reproduced a monotonous image: jowly men perched around the oblong board, docilely ingesting the decrees of their glowering chairman.

That perennial image of corporate directors has been sharpened perceptibly by post-Watergate revelations of management chicanery. With such a diversity of slush funds, bribes, kickbacks and illegal political payments confessed to by hundreds of U.S. managements, even the most experienced directors were exposed as comatose or innocent dupes unwilling to question management, beguiled and deceived by their CEOs. All too clearly, thousands of directors had incontrovertibly demonstrated their characteristic incapacity for discharging their legal responsibility for managing the managers.

Directors should be grateful that their plight has been so widely exposed. For the disclosures have brought them more serious attention than they have ever before enjoyed. Articles, books, seminars and speeches have pondered their predicament, while congressmen and federal agencies—most especially the SEC—have undertaken lengthy investigations.

Research organizations like the Conference Board and the American Society of Corporate Secretaries have analyzed and surveyed directors, while chief executives and even directors themselves have delivered their own judgments.

All these findings, conclusions and recommendations are too profuse to be summarized here. But two opposing views emerge: those outside of management urge stricter control of management and directors by laws and regulating agencies, while those inside management—or dependently associated with it—recommend changing procedures, primarily to secure more "independent" directors and, having secured them, to keep them informed.

What is conspicuously absent from practically all of the proposals is the idea that directors should challenge the dominant position of management. Although CEOs are legally their subordinates, directors still almost universally reject the suggestion that they should remain wary of management and consistently critical of its behavior. Their favorite euphemism is that there should be no "adversary relationship" between themselves and the CEO. However, their insistence on this point is not entirely the product of gentility or traditional docility. It stems basically from the two flat contradictions in the present role of directors: they are given responsibility for managing the corporation and, simultaneously, are deprived of the means—objective, critical information—by which to do so.

Very few directors have spoken out against their common subservience to management and their failure to acquire the means to critically question the CEO, disagree with him and sack him if he fails to perform. Out of bitter experience Louis W. Cabot, chairman of the Cabot Corporation and one of the misled directors held responsible for the bankruptcy of the

Penn Central Railroad in 1970, has written: "A director must be prepared to pass judgment on men who may be his personal friends, or to stomach the responsibility of acting on his critical divergence from management practices when this becomes necessary." But the prevailing attitude of directors was expressed by one who discovered that his friend the CEO was incompetent: "Joe is a nice guy, and removing him is something I just don't want to get into. I'd simply prefer to quietly disappear from the board."

It is significant, therefore, that the author of this book is a director who is prepared to protest what he calls "the management takeover." He is well aware that managing the CEO is no simple proposition and he describes a complex of factors ranging from the proxy system and interlocking directorates to the SEC's rules and the prospects for federal chartering and co-determination. In addition, he has assessed a variety of solutions that have been advanced to alleviate the director's plight.

Two of these "prescriptions" are particularly notable for they deal with areas so sensitive they are ignored by directors as well as by CEOs. One is the scorecard which the author has developed for rating top management; the other is the proposal that boards of directors set up their own staffs to keep them independently informed of management's performance. Theoretically, the adoption of these two procedures might cure all the ills directors are heir to. But neither one is looked on favorably. A separate staff for the board is still condemned by directors because they feel it would establish that "adversary relationship." And CEOs have been consistently scornful of directors' efforts to appraise management's performance. As one described his directors: "They don't know the problem and have no way of deciding whether I do a good job of solving it or not."

This verdict is only a partial truth. There *are* ways by which directors could learn to judge the performance of CEOs. Management, however, has understandably shown little interest in a fully informed, judicious board, and has wanted no interference from an uninformed board. As every CEO knows, the real issue is power: by excluding the board from participating intelligently in the decision-making process, the CEO secures the control he has assumed over the corporation.

These will remain immutable facts of corporate management unless directors change their ways and reclaim at least some of their authority. And there are signs that this might actually happen. Many more directors have begun to take their responsibilities seriously now that their liabilities are growing with every new congressional investigation, stockholder proposal, SEC rule and court decision that affects them. They can expect these outside pressures to increase, for, as SEC Commissioner Williams has pointedly said, "If business cannot clean its own house, government will clean the house of business." A great deal of that cleaning, as the reader of this book will discover, could be done in a hurry if directors put their minds to it.

Preface

Those who become directors of large, publicly held corporations today are the forgotten citizens of the U.S. business world. Legally they are responsible for managing the affairs of their corporations; actually they are selected, elected and dominated by the chief executives of management, who have long since taken over the direction and control of most large corporations. These are the facts that underlie everything presented in this book. They explain both the dilemma of the "outside" director and why the "inside" director, being part of management, has no dilemma.

After thirty years as a director on a score of boards, I look back now to the time I joined my first board and can scarcely believe I was so innocent and unprepared for what lay ahead. I thought I knew, as a student of management since the middle 1920s, what it took to be a director. Not only was I surprised to learn that there was no "job description" for directors, but my colleagues on that first board were visibly startled that I should raise the question.

Nevertheless, as a young consultant I was anxious to be a "good" director. So privately and respectfully I asked an experienced and distinguished fellow director for advice. He told me straight out, "Go along with management. Ask only convenient questions and don't rock the boat." Today, countless board meetings later, I still think that is the best description of a "good" director I have ever heard. And, I regret to say, I don't know a single chief executive who wouldn't agree emphatically.

After a little firsthand experience, however, being a "good" director didn't satisfy me. I wanted to be a "better" director and thought I might find clues to how to do this in the New York and Delaware corporation laws and in the bylaws of the company itself. It was a rather dry study. The corporation laws and bylaws all said about the same thing, that a "corporation shall be managed by a board of directors consisting of one or more members." I could find no responsibilities or duties listed or suggested. Disillusioned by this meager guidance, I concluded that corporation laws, like all other laws, had been drawn by lawyers for lawyers so that you had to hire a lawyer to get an interpretation that could be both questionable and expensive.

I turned from the law and began combing management literature, biographies and news reports. By then I was looking for clues as to how to be an "effective" director, since this was the kind of director many were recommending. I found numerous lists outlining the responsibilities of a director, but not one of them told me *how* to become an effective director.

I continued my search every time I went abroad and studied the "co-determination" movement in Europe. The two-tier boards—representing both management and labor—in West German companies fascinated me, and I think this is probably a pattern we may all be moving toward. Companies in England, Holland and Belgium, under the pressure of labor unions, are already moving toward the adoption of two-tier boards. In France and Switzerland boards are highly restricted by law, and Sweden has passed a law that gives the government the right to appoint one director to every corporate board.

The evolution of the European boards, however, has not indicated how one might be an effective director in the industrial system in the United States. Although I am going to keep looking, my search so far has convinced me that no listing or theory will give me the answers I seek. The more I see, hear and do as a director, the more I am forced to conclude that the process of becoming an effective director must be a do-it-yourself program.

My own program isn't complicated, but it isn't simple, either; to understand it a reader ought to be aware of the complex issues and problems facing directors today—and that's what most of this book is about.

EDWARD MCSWEENEY

1

The Director's Sorry Lot

The Management Takeover

The status of corporate directors has been deteriorating for nearly a century; today, in the late 1970s, it seems to have reached its lowest point. Directors have been repeatedly exposed as silent or deceived partners in elusive and fraudulent practices of management; they have sat by while management took huge industrial complexes into bankruptcy; they have condoned the payment of bribes and kickbacks; they have refused to demand the resignations of irresponsible and incompetent executives. By such sins of omission, directors have shown that they have indeed become pawns of management.

Today many directors are casual, many irresponsible, many confused and timid and many neither anxious nor curious about their responsibilities and the liabilities they may incur. But others are worried. Court decisions, legislation and rulings of the Securities and Exchange Commission in recent years have made many think twice about serving on a board of directors. Some are now flatly refusing to do so —and this is a new and significant development in the evolution of the corporate director.

The character of the director has gone through three major transformations since U.S. corporations were first chartered by the states in the 1830s. In the first phase, which lasted about fifty years, corporations remained relatively small and were closely controlled by a few stockholders who, being the owners, were eager to set company policies and manage its operations. These were usually family companies run by fathers, sons, relatives and in-laws who, as directors-owners-managers, looked carefully after the business. Management and ownership were one.

Thousands of family owned and managed companies still exist, and family control through stock ownership is dominant today in companies bearing such familiar names as Du Pont, Ford, Heinz, Reynolds and Mellon as well as in countless other, smaller corporations. In 1967 *Fortune* found that 30 percent of those on its list of the 500 largest industrials were "clearly controlled by identifiable individuals, or by family groups." Although even in these companies management generally has a powerful if not dominant voice, major decisions are still made by directors representing the interests of the controlling stockholders. (These are not the casual directors who are the concern of this book.)

The idea that management was something to be studied and practiced did not occur to owner-directors until long after the Civil War. Those who helped to supervise businesses were simply "hired hands" who had no voice in management. The first "student's business school" was started by a retired army man, General Robert E. Lee, when he was president of what is now Washington and Lee University. But that experiment expired with Lee's death, and it was not until 1881 that the Wharton School was founded at the University of Pennsylvania through the generosity of an ironmaster, Joseph Wharton.

By that time, however, the character of the corporate director had already begun to change. As companies had grown and come to need more capital, they sold more and more stock to the public, and the close control of the owner-directors gave way to control by the financiers. Investment bankers, led by J. P. Morgan, assumed seats on the boards of scores of corporations; through trusts and mergers financed by other people's money they built a binding web of interlocking directorates. With the financier-directors boldly concentrating on manipulating stocks for profit, management was for the most part ignored and the other members of such boards were usually prominent figureheads chosen to impress investors (and they were known, quite accurately, as "dummy directors"). The financier-director was curbed to some extent by antitrust laws, but interlocking directorates continued to give bankers, lawyers and insurance companies undisputed control over the management of most large corporations until after World War I.

During the 1920s the "hired hands" began to come to power. The swift expansion of mass production and mass marketing required a new breed of manager who had the expertise to put the U.S. economy into high gear. The managers became indispensable and were increasingly respected by directors who began to pay them their first large salaries. By this time, too, the stockholders of most large companies had become so numerous and so dispersed that virtually none of them thought of themselves as owners.

Instead, as investors and speculators, they looked for better dividends or quick profits and were little concerned with management decisions. Like the outside directors, they were content to let management run things, aware that they themselves would never know enough to be able to do so. Ownership of the corporation thus became divorced from control of its operations, that is, from management.

The first definitive statement of these facts, with supporting statistics, appeared in 1932 in *The Modern Corporation and Private Property* by A. A. Berle and Gardiner C. Means: by 1929 44 percent of the 200 largest corporations were controlled by management. Not until nearly thirty years later, however, were their findings generally accepted. "Almost everyone now agrees," economist Edward S. Mason wrote in 1959, "that in the large corporation, the owner is, in general, a passive recipient of income, that, typically, control is in the hands of management, and that management selects its own replacements." In 1963 a study by R. J. Larner showed that 84 percent of the 200 largest corporations were controlled by management.

The management takeover was called "the managerial revolution" by Berle and Means, who thought it meant corporations would become so "socialized" that managers would tend to act like public servants and would not work to maximize profits. No revolution of this kind ever occurred; if anything, managers have become even hungrier for money and power than the free enterprisers.

Management nailed down its control of the large corporation by taking charge of the proxy system of electing directors. Chief executives name the candidates they want on their boards and, through proxies signed by apathetic stockholders, insure their nearly unanimous election. Those who are elected almost invariably re-elect the executives who chose them. Thus management has become, in Berle's words, "a self-perpetuating oligarchy."

With management firmly in the saddle, the corporate director has come to be seen as a legalistic anachronism and has tended to be casual about his responsibilities under lenient state laws. How heavily directors have relied on management was demonstrated repeatedly during the 1960s when management's drive for "growth" and increased earnings started a flood of mergers that swept thousands of small corporations into the arms of huge conglomerates. Often these deals were achieved with the aid of questionable practices recommended by accounting firms hired by management. All too often the directors involved were told little or nothing—and were typically too timid or too loyal to question management's judgment and decisions.

The carelessness of directors and the extravagance of management should come as no surprise to those who recall the astute observations of the first great champion of free enterprise. Two hundred years ago Adam Smith expressed his low opinion of both the owners and the managers of joint stock companies. Most owners, he wrote, "seldom pretend to understand anything of the business of the company," while the managers could not be expected to watch over other people's money with the "anxious vigilance" of private business partners. He concluded that "negligence and profusion, therefore, must always prevail, more or less, in the management of the affairs of such a company." To Adam Smith, managers were known as "directors"; he did not foresee that this word would later be applied to the trustees appointed by owners to oversee the managers—or that the managers would one day overcome their overseers.

The dominance of management was inevitable once ownership became divorced from operating control and corporations had grown so big and complex that directors could not possibly know enough to manage them. As it was, the hired hands the directors depended on had to teach themselves. And the results comprise one of the most remarkable chapters in the history of education. Ever since the pre-World War I days of Frederick Winslow Taylor, the father of "scientific management" through work measurement and job descriptions, management has learned and learned, not only about engineering, production and marketing but also about itself. Now the study of management techniques and executive development takes place in many forums, from seminars and refresher courses (such as those of the American Management Association) to the extensive programs of business schools that are now found at over 200 colleges and universities.

With all its know-how and its power over others, management has kept itself singularly free from interference by outsiders. It has remained accountable to no authority other than its own judgment and the personal ethics of its top executives. In the past only reformers and agitators considered this to be a bad thing; the public in general has accepted management's totalitarian status and conceded that its primary goal, the maximization of profits, is usually to society's benefit.

Today, however, more of the public than ever before are demanding that management be held socially responsible for its actions wherever these are detrimental to the public interest. Almost overnight, corporate directors have been faced with a wide range of challenges and problems they had assumed were strictly *not* their responsibility: housing, urban renewal, community welfare, medical care, education, juvenile delinquency and, most emphatically, environmental pollution. There appear to be no simple solutions for these problems, nor does there appear to be a formula that can solve the central, critical issue: How can the corporation's need for profits be combined with the needs of society?

It is clear that the capitalistic system in the large corporation has been going astray for a considerable time. The laws governing corporations have long since been nullified by the realities of the management takeover. Stockholders now blindly elect directors whom management has selected, and directors more or less blindly approve what management does in its own interests. Fearful of offending management, directors decline to perform their most essential function, that of critically reviewing management's plans, policies and strategies and continually appraising its performance.

No one knows what will become of the corporate director. There are signs that drastic changes in his role may be forthcoming. The spread of conglomerates and multinational corporate empires is steadily increasing the pressure for stiffer laws and regulations to hold directors and officers more accountable for their decisions. And reformers have again raised the old demand (rejected by the Founding Fathers) that the federal government take over the chartering of corporations so that all companies might be subject to a uniform set of controls and penalties.

Before such reforms are accomplished, however, there is the possibility that a new kind of director—the institutional director—may come to dominate the decisions of management. The assets of pension and mutual funds, bank trusts and insurance companies have been estimated at over one trillion dollars, and already some of their holdings are big enough to insure voting control of some very large corporations and strong influence in a great many others.

So far, the managers of the institutional funds have declined to interfere with management. They have accepted management's control and its decisions, preferring, like the ordinary stockholder, to sell their holdings when management fails to produce satisfactory earnings. Should these fund managers seriously begin to control management decisions, history might repeat itself in the reappearance of the dummy directors of the days of J. P. Morgan, directors accountable only to anonymous financiers concerned solely with financial gain.

Finally, there is the possibility that large corporations will operate openly as partners of the government, with management collaborating with state and federal regulating agencies even more closely than it does now. The result could be a kind of industrial state socialism in which management-appointed directors would either disappear altogether or remain as legal holdovers, rubberstamping the joint decisions of management and government and having no more anxieties about their responsibilities or liabilities. Many directors today might find this a welcome relief.

Directors: Pro and Con

One may well conclude from all that has been said and written about directors of large corporations that they are of little or no importance and are perhaps unnecessary. But state laws still make them legally responsible for managing the corporation, and they continue to be elected. In fact there

is a good deal to be said for—as well as against—the corporate director, and consequently there has been a continuous,
general confusion.

There are, basically, three kinds of directors: the original
kind, the twentieth-century kind and the mixed breed. The
original kind is the director of a private corporation, a "family" corporation, dominated and controlled by one, two or
three families. No one knows how many of these there are;
only those with more than 500 stockholders and assets over
one million dollars are required to disclose their figures to the
SEC.

The mixed-breed director is found on the boards of semiprivate corporations. These multiplied quickly during the
bull market of the 1960s when "going public" looked good
to many private "family" companies. In most cases, however, working control was kept in the hands of the original
stockholders; although the companies' stocks are listed publicly, their directors are essentially the same as those of the
"family" corporations (i.e., they are both the owners *and* the
managers of their companies).

The third kind of director—what can be called the twentieth-century variety, though they first appeared toward the
end of the nineteenth century—is native to the boardrooms
of the large, publicly held corporation. Here the directors
may own no stock at all, and no director, officer or stockholder usually owns more than a fraction of one percent of
all the shares outstanding. The corporations they serve are
now far richer and far bigger, and they affect millions of
people and consume enormously greater resources than all
the private and semiprivate companies put together. It is the
directors of large public corporations who appear to be the
last hope of keeping the American free enterprise system

operating without succumbing to total control by government agencies.

There is a lot to be said for the "dummy director," and it is no accident that such directors have continued to flourish as the silent stooges of management. The rubber-stamp director has been the mainstay of the large corporation; he is the director who will remain mute for hours in a board meeting, listening servilely or tolerantly while the chief executive tells the board what he proposes to do—or has already done without first telling the directors. The puppet director is the easy target of economists, sociologists and cartoonists —and all those who will never be asked to join a board of directors. He is not, however, to be laughed at openly if you are the chief executive.

The fact is that without thousands of dummy directors ready to rubberstamp the actions of top management, the U.S. business world would not be what it is today. For these directors have let the chief executives and their staffs run things as they saw best—and the unchecked decisions of management have been spectacularly successful in producing an affluent economy without parallel in human history.

The dummy director serves further as "window dressing" to help attract investors to a new or struggling company. Getting the presidents of well-known corporations (or even a former U.S. President like Herbert Hoover) to sit on a board is generally expected to convince both the general public and speculators that the company is "sound." This ancient and universal practice bears no relation to the real status of directors, but it does indicate the faith that even chief executives have in the image of the director.

Directors have also been useful to many outside the corporation. Lawyers, bankers and state legislators especially have found the corporation to be a treasurehouse of fees and taxes. From the time a few states began chartering corporations "for any lawful purpose" 180 years ago, lawyers have flourished by serving as both counselors and directors on their clients' boards. Bankers lost no time in becoming directors who supplied financial advice and secured, in return, the rewards of handling corporation accounts and the legal paperwork for new issues of stock.

The state legislators probably didn't realize at first how lush a field they were opening up in the corporation chartering business. State after state introduced statutes that authorized enterprising businessmen to issue shares of stock in return for investors' capital, each share carrying the right to vote for a board of directors by whom "the corporation shall be managed." The directors in turn were empowered to elect as officers those whom they could trust to operate the venture in their behalf. As might be expected, major stockholders elected themselves directors and usually appointed themselves the managing officers as well. Thus stockholders prudently secured a three-way grip on their business as directors, officers and managers.

That grip weakened as corporations grew bigger, acquired more stockholders and hired more managers. As the chartering business boomed, states attracted new incorporators to their bailiwicks by reducing the early restrictions in their statutes. New Jersey liberalized its charters so generously between 1888 and 1904 that over half the 354 companies capitalized at more than one million dollars in that period chose to settle there. That state also welcomed trusts and holding companies that other states called illegal.

In 1899 Delaware got into the race in earnest and subsequently so liberalized its charters that today over 80,000

companies, including one-third of those listed on the New
York Stock Exchange, find that state the most amenable
home. Their fees provide one-fourth of Delaware's annual
revenues. Directors were remembered in 1974 when Delaware changed its statute to read that a corporation "shall be
managed by *or under the direction of* a board of directors."
The new (italicized) words finally recognized the long obvious fact that a large corporation today cannot possibly be
managed by its directors.

The many unfavorable things to be reported about corporate directors concern the particular problems, limitations
and failings to which they are heir. In recent years the
charges against them have become insistent and their weaknesses have been shot at from all sides. Since Watergate the
SEC has smoked out political payoffs and bribes by scores of
corporations that directors should have vetoed, yet only a
few of the chief executives involved in these transgressions
have been fired by their boards.

Some critics have tended to excuse the directors, putting
the blame on apathetic stockholders or on pro-management
influences hidden behind the millions of shares held in
"street name" accounts and in pension and trust funds
managed by the banks. Some blame the lax state laws and,
like Ralph Nader, have called for the federal chartering of
corporations. But the central fact remains: directors have let
management take over the controls, select its own loyal,
friendly directors, choose its own successors and set its own
compensation.

How can directors regain some of the authority they have
surrendered to management? Will the blank-check proxy
system ever be changed so as to give directors and stockholders a greater voice in company policies? And will directors
ever muster the courage to perform their most important

task—to appraise, honestly and continuously, the chief executive's performance and replace him if he flunks their examination?

The Three-Horned Dilemma

For many directors there is no dilemma. The inside directors, who are officers and executives subordinate to the chief executive officer, are employees who have no reason to choose. They are constrained to protect their jobs by doing what the CEO expects them to do, that is, to approve whatever he decides and proposes. Failing that, they are separated from the board and the corporation simultaneously. Much the same subservient stance is required of those specialized outside directors—investment bankers, lawyers and other consultants—whose self-interest keeps them in management's service. They are virtually inside directors.

However, for the genuine outside director who is neither a subordinate nor a servant of management, there is a serious dilemma. That dilemma has three horns, but two of the alternatives are so demanding that only the boldest outside directors venture to propose them. Thus the majority of outside directors choose the least painful alternative and accept the same passive role that management expects of inside directors: They go along.

For this passive attitude there is a common explanation. Outside directors decline to discharge their legal responsibility to "manage the corporation" because they know they cannot do what the law says; they don't know enough and can't or won't take the time to learn and appraise what management is doing.

But the rising risks of being sued, of being found guilty of

fraud or negligence, are waking up many outside directors—
and some have begun to grasp the second horn of their
dilemma. This takes courage, for it means changing the director's behavior and his attitude toward management. In
effect it means reestablishing the board's authority over management.

There are many different ways in which this can be done.
Some, such as defining the director's authority and responsibilities and developing a code of ethics, are tentative and
merely preliminary. But some boards have taken sterner
measures, such as establishing an audit committee to check
up on management's financial information and operating
performance and asking management to furnish more information on its plans and policies.

In taking such actions, outside directors are very likely to
cool their relationship with the CEO and with inside directors as well. A director who proposes a change that is voted
down can expect to become an undesirable candidate for
re-election to the board. Two possible board actions are so
threatening to management that few directors are even willing to discuss them: changing the proxy system and setting
standards for appraising management's performance.

The third horn of the outside director's dilemma has
scarcely been recognized among U.S. directors. This involves
changing the corporate hierarchy to allow nonmanagement
employees to participate in the decision-making process, and
in Europe is known as co-determination.

Regardless of the actions U.S. directors may take to re-
solve their dilemma, it seemed fairly certain in 1978 that
Congress would finally enact legislation to restrict management's dominance of board business. And eventually some
form of federal chartering could drastically change the traditional procedures and attitudes of all boards.

2

The Nature of the Species

Who Is Qualified to Be a Director?

There are practically no legal barriers to becoming a director of a large public corporation in the United States. State laws —with the exception of New York and New Jersey statutes which stipulate that one must be twenty-one years of age— do not define or limit the qualifications for board membership. And the only federal regulations are those involving security clearances required by the Defense Department for directors serving on the boards of multinational corporations that have overseas subsidiaries and do classified work.

Nevertheless, a great many restrictions on board membership exist, and these are extremely strict. Women, blacks and members of other minority groups were disqualified until recent years, when a few "cosmetic" directors began to be elected for the sake of political and public relations. The really significant fact is that all but a few business and professional men fail to qualify as candidates for board membership.

33

The reason for this pronounced discrimination is no deep secret: directors are nearly always chosen and/or approved by the chief executive officer. His personal preferences, his idiosyncracies and his desire to secure control of the board together rule out all but that particular handful of candidates who will be compatible with him.

Thus the single most important qualification of a director is to be a loyal friend of the chief executive, one who will regularly support and approve his decisions, plans and recommendations. A director's loyalty is most certain when he happens to be an employee; this ordinarily means a subordinate officer or a senior executive whose status and future career in the company are dependent on his relationship to the CEO.

The *officer-director* is the inside director par excellence; he offers no criticisms of his boss and is always ready to approve his plans and decisions, even when these may seriously affect his own career. Some boards are composed entirely of such captive directors, though the trend toward having more outside directors has probably reduced the number of such companies.

The second most important qualification for a directorship is that the candidate himself be a chief executive. The experience of the CEO-director as a peer of the CEO is expected to reinforce his loyalty by making him generally sympathetic to the man who has to explain things to a board. Today, however, a good many chief executives are declining invitations to join boards. Some say they are too busy with their own problems to help solve another company's difficulties; others frankly admit that the liabilities are now too great for those who cannot spare the time to exercise "due diligence" in dealing with another company's problems. But the time-honored practice of reciprocal directorships continues, based firmly on the ancient proposition, "you scratch my back, and I'll scratch yours." Chief executives who swap board memberships are within the law so long as their companies do not serve the same markets. However, the risk of a conflict of interest is always present, and it takes constant surveillance to avoid it.

The third general qualification for becoming a director is to be a professional or technical specialist who is both compatible with the CEO and expert on matters concerning the corporation. This category, composed mainly of individuals in the fields of finance, law, accounting, consulting and education, is the largest source of candidates for board membership. Theoretically, all of these candidates become outside directors; in practice, many are so close to the CEO, or have interests so closely identified with those of the corporation, that they function as inside directors.

The qualifications of the following so-called "outside" directors not only vary considerably but are also beginning to change. To wit:

Men of finance historically have played dominant roles in the affairs of corporate boards, as the activities of John Pierpont Morgan and his successors have demonstrated. More recently, financial advisors and money managers have joined the commercial and investment bankers who sit on major corporation boards. The *financier-director* generally has direct (and usually very profitable) commercial relations with the corporation—lending capital, underwriting stock issues and handling financial deals. These interests scarcely allow them to be labeled outside directors.

Among the financiers, as among the chief executives asked to join boards, there is now a growing reluctance to serve as directors. Investment bankers are no longer so anxious to sit in on board meetings as they were in the post-World War II days of the renowned Sidney Weinberg of Goldman Sachs, who once served simultaneously on 34 corporate boards. His successor, the late Gus Levy, served on 19 boards—but he was an exception, for the watchdog activities of the SEC and other agencies have discouraged many from accepting directorships. At the same time, there has been the realization among other kinds of directors that having an investment banker on the board tends to stifle competition from other investment houses that might better supply the corporation's needs. Thus a financier-director can hurt the corporation while serving his own interests.

Members of the legal profession cherish the directorships they hold on the boards of their clients. There is perhaps no better way for a lawyer to secure the close relationships with corporation officers that will benefit his firm. Rarely does the lawyer-director give much thought to the possibility that the corporation may thereby find itself limited in the breadth and quality of the legal advice it receives.

In view of their patent self-interest, it is hard to justify lawyers as corporate directors. True, they can provide board meetings with instant legal counsel on some technicalities and legislative problems; but the difficult issues that face a board require deliberate counsel that any lawyer should be glad to furnish, at his regular fees, orally or in writing to the board. Indeed, there is scarcely more justification for putting a lawyer on a board than for giving a directorship to the specialist who handles the corporation's computer equipment.

That self-interest inevitably impairs the judgment of specialist directors is even more true in the case of a corporation's general counsel, who so often automatically becomes a board member. If he is a close friend of the CEO, there is the strong possibility that he will end up running the CEO and shaping his decisions—at his own usual hourly rates. He can become the only inside director with power.

The *accountant-director* is less common today; perhaps his qualifications have always been suspect. The largest accounting firms, through serious brushes with the SEC and adverse court decisions, have learned the risks of having a partner as a director of a client corporation. In other cases, the ability of an accountant-director to be objective about a board's decisions when it is his own firm's financial statements that he is reviewing, interpreting and approving is certainly to be doubted.

The *consultant-director* in many cases is another flawed candidate for board membership. He may be naturally inclined to focus on the single objective that is his particular speciality—such as management reorganization—which may not be at all what the corporation really needs. And while serving on the board of one client he is likely to develop a major conflict of interest as a director advising the boards of other clients.

The *educator-director* usually does not face conflict of interest problems. Indeed, chief executives today are increasingly interested in securing as directors those who are the heads of educational and scientific institutions, for their names and reputations can reflect favorably on the corporation's image. Less glamorous professors and department heads are also now popular candidates for board memberships, especially when they can provide expertise in an area —such as economics or sociology—that could prove important to the corporation. At the same time, the educator-director generally comes from the academic world with little or no experience or knowledge of the business world. He may therefore propose ideas concerning social issues, consumers or management that are unrealistic, impractical or naive— yet he may be so venerated a figure that even these opinions are accepted as reliable.

Usually a retired executive or government employee, the *"professional" director* may often call himself a "working" director and may spend his full time serving on the boards of several companies. Frequently he contributes significantly to a board's deliberations. However, he is not a professional and cannot be until qualifications and standards for directors are generally or legally established and consistently enforced by a jury of peers who pass on a candidate's qualifications. That state of affairs is still a long way off.

The *cosmetic director* is one selected by a CEO or an influential stockholder in the hope of improving the corporation's image as a broadminded, socially conscious, humanitarian organization. This director is a woman, a black or a member of some other minority group, and, as such, his or her qualifications to be a director are simply not valid. The selection of such directors is rarely founded on their business competence or knowledge; instead they are elected in the curious belief that each will represent the interests of his or her particular minority. This is an absurd distortion of the purposes of board membership; every director in a large corporation should represent the interests of many different groups—stockholders, bondholders, employees, consumers, local communities, the general public—that have a stake in the corporation, and each director should take considerable care not to favor one group at the expense of another.

The qualifications of the ideal director have not yet been

established, and they may never be. Presumably such a director would be qualified to: (a) act as a trustee charged with protecting and increasing the corporation's physical and human assets; (b) contribute to the balance of a board in which each member makes particular contributions of knowledge, experience and expertise; (c) use the board membership to advance the interests of the corporation, not those of the individual director; (d) see that each director's time was paid for at the same hourly rate earned by the chief executive; and (e) forbid the board to be used to advance the CEO's interests.

Clearly these are not the qualifications for board membership that chief executives have required of candidates. And the CEO's criteria will persist until directors are willing to assume their responsibility for selecting candidates for election to the board who will manage, and not be managed by, the chief executive.

Why Directors Take the Risks

While the risk of liability as a corporate director have gone up drastically in recent years, there are still a lot of very satisfying things to be enjoyed as a board member of a large corporation.

- *Prestige.* The ego-soothing satisfaction of belonging to one of the most exclusive fraternities in business has long been the most powerful lure. Election to the board of a big corporation confers a status unattainable in ordinary executive and professional life.
- *Interlocks.* Fellow directors include executives, bank-

ers, insurance men and professionals who serve on the boards of other large corporations and are thus good sources of economic and strategic business information.

- *Business know-how.* Dealing with the problems and methods of large corporations can improve a director's ability to handle those of his own company.
- *Inside information.* Board discussions frequently reveal significant data about an industry or another corporation that a director can make use of.
- *Financial gain.* Corporations that give directors stock options may provide board members with sizable capital gains—providing they avoid the risks of "insider trading."
- *Enhanced career.* The directorship of a prominent corporation can reflect credit on a director's own corporation and at the same time improve both his image and his opportunities for advancement either within or outside his own company.
- *Challenges.* The problems of another corporation may offer a director the chance to demonstrate capacities and skills not called for in his own company.
- *Friendships.* A director can develop personal ties with other successful people that may open for him new and fruitful business and social opportunities.
- *Fees or retainers.* Considerably sweetened in recent years, these now range from $100 a day plus expenses to $30,000 or more a year.
- *Perks.* A few corporations now provide directors with extra rewards or perquisites—but such rewards are still small compared to management's.

The Disadvantages of Being a Director

Most businessmen now take a very hard look at any invitation to stand for election to a board of directors. They are especially wary of the liabilities a director may face under the rulings of the SEC, the Justice Department and the courts. And there are a lot of other reasons for anxiety.

- *Time required.* With more corporations increasing the amount of data submitted to their directors, a board member can expect to spend from several hours to several days reading and preparing for each board meeting.
- *Lack of critical information.* Intent on preventing criticism of their performance, most chief executives carefully tailor or otherwise limit the data they provide their directors on the corporation's most serious problems. While some boards now have their own audit committees, few if any corporate boards have yet been provided with their own information-gathering staffs.
- *Submission to management.* Chief executives of large corporations habitually expect directors to be passive and to approve without serious questioning management's plans, strategies and policies.
- *The CEO's idiosyncracies.* Directors often have to put up with peculiar demands and prejudices of a dominant CEO. For example, they may have to eat the CEO's favorite food at all board luncheons and refrain from smoking in his presence; they may have to forgo buying or driving any car made outside the United States.
- *Criticizing the CEO.* Directors who persistently ask probing questions about management and find fault with or vote against its policies are rarely welcome on

a board. Compatibility with management ordinarily means meek acceptance of what the CEO wants.

- *Appraising management.* Judging openly the performance of the CEO and his senior officers is so delicate a business that it is almost never attempted. A director who proposes a careful, specific review of management's record and its objectives is not likely to be considered for re-election.
- *Firing the CEO.* This is the most disagreeable task of the board; it not only hurts the CEO, it reflects on the board's capacity for overseeing and controlling management's performance. Directors generally choose to resign rather than demand the CEO's resignation.
- *Cliques.* Nearly all boards include one or more groups of directors—often but not always officer-directors—who side constantly with management and may keep to themselves important inside information that management doesn't want the rest of the board to have.
- *Embarrassing directors.* There is frequently at least one board member who is capable of damaging the corporate image and distressing his fellow directors. He is often a senile founder-director who sleeps through meetings, but he may be a once-renowned executive who has lost both his status and his grasp of current corporate problems. Another type is the "token" director who pushes the claims of a minority group without understanding the complexities of the situation.
- *Poor pay.* In spite of increases in fees and retainers paid by some large corporations today, directors on the whole are stingily rewarded for the time and effort they should be expending in fulfilling their responsibilities.

Duties and Responsibilities

Directors, who have a long tradition of being heedless of their responsibilities, are now paying sharp attention to the subject. Nothing disturbs a director more than the threat of being sued for negligence or fraud, and since the disastrous bankruptcy of the Penn Central in 1970 stockholders and the law have been coming down hard on negligent directors. Directors who formerly left everything to the chief executive are now anxious to learn what their specific duties and responsibilities are under the law.

It is still a very murky business. State corporation laws are practically no help. With amazingly similar wording, they state broadly that the corporation "shall be managed by a board of directors who shall be elected by the stockholders." Delaware has expanded on this somewhat, but it still takes a lawsuit to pry from the courts what is meant by a director's legal liability in each case.

Fortunately for directors, the courts have been lenient as to what constitutes negligence on a director's part. The "prudent man" rule remains the best umbrella under which directors may escape the thrust of stockholder suits. A director who can show he acted in "good faith," used "due diligence" in making a "reasonable investigation" of the facts and acted like "a prudent man in the management of his own property" is about as safe as he can expect to be from being found guilty of negligence.

Nevertheless a lot of directors are uneasy and are trying hard to clear away the haze that surrounds their responsibilities. Some have drawn up elaborate, lengthy lists of functions expected of the board; in one case the list runs to more than sixty different items. The actions specified in these lists often cover so much ground that—theoretically—there would be little left for management to handle. One such list contains twenty-three verbs: review, interpret, implement, assist, evaluate, approve, select, elect, compensate, appoint, terminate, advise, deliberate, examine, be informed, be sensitive, warn, change, issue, decide, execute, recommend and establish. These earnest efforts to nail down the board's responsibilities, however, often omit critically important functions. The responsibility to submit management's actions and plans to hard, critical questioning is rarely mentioned.

Some directors have gone to the other extreme and boiled their responsibilities down to a few functions. One poll of sophisticated directors reduced the list to one legal function —their fiduciary responsibility (for preserving company assets, etc.)—and four items involving the chief executive: hiring him, compensating him fairly, helping him (if requested) and firing him (if necessary). This simplified listing of priorities is illusory. Directors in fact are not held to strict fiduciary responsibility beyond the legal actions cited in their companies' charters—such as declaring dividends, issuing shares and changing bylaws. And directors rarely hire or fire a chief executive, often overcompensate him and seldom are asked to help him.

It is scarcely surprising that even the Securities and Exchange Commission abandoned its attempt to define the responsibilities of directors. Still, the effort to define the director's tasks can be worthwhile: It can reveal how little help the law affords, and it often leads to interesting conclusions. A director might discover, for example, that for his own protection the appointment of subcommittees of the board can be very useful. One of the best moves a board can make is to set up an audit committee that reports directly to the board—and engages its own auditing firm.

Another prudent move for any director who is alert to the risks of his position is to keep himself well posted on current federal legislation. He should be particularly careful to watch for changes in his responsibilities. He should have spotted, for example, that striking statement in the new federal regulations of ERISA (Employee Retirement Income Security Act) which cover corporate pension plans, where, for the first time, directors *and* officers are held specifically liable for failure to enforce the regulations.

There will almost certainly be more of the same. As federal regulations and court decisions become more sophisticated, directors who want to sharpen their own guidelines will need considerable courage. The essential first step should be to separate and define clearly the differences between the chief executive's responsibilities and those of the board chairman. Then the board will have the makings of a "scorecard" to measure the chief executive's performance. And that, after all, is their first and greatest responsibility.

3

Management's Trump Card

The Blank Check Proxy System

The proxy system assures management of control over the directors and the voting stockholders of large public corporations; it is the biggest weapon management has for perpetuating itself, its policies and its handpicked, cooperative directors. The system makes a mockery of the longstanding myth that the stockholders select and elect the directors to manage the corporation. The myth is a relic of "stockholder democracy," a hand-me-down from the days when entrepreneurs put up the money as owners-directors-managers under the law of property rights. The law assumed that stockholders actually owned the corporation, and the stockholder who didn't show up at a stockholders' meeting had to sign a proxy that handed over his voting rights to the others (i.e., he was penalized for being absent).

But this system lost its meaning when corporations grew big and their stockholders became scattered across the coun-

try. No longer owner-managers but now investors and
speculators, the stockholders abdicated en masse, leaving the
corporation to the hired managers. The managers gained
control without ownership by taking charge of the proxy
system.

The system is now routine. Stockholders who cannot or
will not attend a stockholders' meeting are asked to sign a
proxy form naming two or three agents to vote their shares
in their absence. In this the directors are bypassed; the proxy
form clearly states that it is "solicited by management." It
is management that (1) appoints the proxy agents who serve
as dummies to vote as management instructs, (2) selects the
candidates it wants elected as directors and (3) specifies the
propositions or actions it wants approved. Thus management
acquires a blank check for everything it needs to preserve its
control and perpetuate its tenure.

The stockholder is left with three alternatives. He can stick
to the role of market gambler and ignore the proxy, selling
his stock if he thinks the company is in trouble or he sees a
better gamble elsewhere. Or he can trust management absolutely, signing the proxy and handing over his votes to the
dummy agents. Or he can act as an interested owner, taking
the trouble to attend stockholders' meetings and cast his
votes in person.

The only time management seriously cares what the stockholder does is when its tenure is threatened by a proxy fight
stirred up by stockholders or a tender offer engineered by a
raider who seeks control of the corporation. Otherwise the
blank-check proxy system gives management an overwhelming advantage over stockholders who attempt to change its
policies or the composition of the board. Management usually holds enough proxies to insure that 95 to 99 percent of

the votes are cast in favor of its propositions and its slate of directors.

This happens not just because any one stockholder of a large corporation today rarely holds more than a fraction of one percent of all shares outstanding; the real source of management's leverage lies in those enormous blocks of stock held in countless funds—pension, insurance mutual, money management, trust, foundation, religious—and the millions of additional shares held for other "beneficial owners" whose names are thoroughly disguised. The proxy system assures that practically all these absentee voters support management's ticket. No dictator ever had more absolute control over his subjects.

Democracy Versus the Proxy

While the directors of a large public corporation are legally vulnerable to attack at any stockholders' meeting, they have little to worry about. Court decisions and SEC restrictions have severely crimped and blunted the stockholder's chief weapon, the proxy ballot. Most stockholders themselves don't want to use it—which indicates how powerfully stockholders have been imbued with the doctrine that management has a "right" not to be interfered with or criticized.

Still there are signs that "shareholder democracy" is not dead. Year after year a small band of professional gadflies stands up at annual meetings to question, criticize, make demands of and argue with board chairmen and directors about the management of their corporations. The names of the most persistent of these zealots—John and Lewis Gilbert, Wilma Soss, Evelyn Davis—are better known than those of most of today's conglomerates. And experience has made them successful in getting their proposals on a corporation's proxy ballot.

This is no small accomplishment. While the 1933 federal securities laws originally gave stockholders the right to submit proxy proposals to management, the SEC has subsequently placed narrow limits on what may actually be submitted to the stockholders. Thus management can refuse to accept a proposal for the proxy if it (1) is submitted mainly "for the purpose of promoting general economic, political, racial, religious, social or similar causes" or (2) asks management to do something about "the ordinary business operations" of the corporation.

A proposal must be carefully drawn to qualify for inclusion on a proxy ballot. Proposals concerning dividend payments, advertising policies, the selling of a subsidiary and the desegregation of buses have been invalidated. Those that have passed the tests have generally been drafted by the professional gadflies and have dealt with such matters as voting rights, directors' terms, annual meetings, executive compensation, pensions and stock options. Only a few social issues—primarily pollution and military contracts—manage to gain attention at annual meetings of large corporations.

Community groups have occasionally forced management to change its policies. In Rochester, New York, a group called FIGHT, using a variety of tactics, eventually got Kodak to change its minority hiring policy. But proxies were not critical in that decision; the proxies withheld from management were less than one percent of the 161 million shares outstanding.

Campaign GM, a highly publicized shareholder effort started by Ralph Nader in 1970, managed to get SEC approval for only two of nine proposals it recommended that year. One of the two asked that three "public representatives" be added to General Motors' board; the other proposed a stockholders' "Committee for Corporate Responsibility." These won the votes of less than 3 percent of GM's 285 million shares. GM's directors later decided to establish a public policy committee of the board and a vice presidency of environmental activities; it also appointed Leon Sullivan, a prominent black minister, to the board.

In the following year Sullivan split the board by publicly supporting a proposal to end GM's operations in Africa. Even so, management won nearly 99 percent of the votes on the issue. In 1972 not one of the nine stockholder proposals got enough votes (3 percent of the total) to qualify for reintroduction at the 1973 meeting, at which time six other proposals shared the same fate. After that, Campaign GM came to an end.

The overwhelming disinterest of stockholders in such efforts was evident in the attitudes of those responsible for voting the substantial holdings of institutions—particularly universities and foundations—to whom Campaign GM had appealed. Many large universities voted with management, and others dumped their stock to avoid controversy. Only a few small colleges backed the proposals.

A vote of 5 percent against a management proposal is still rare, and no stockholder proposal has yet come anywhere near winning even a respectable minority of proxy ballots. However, one proposal offered to the stockholders of one utility corporation in 1976 received a surprising 11 percent of the votes cast. Significantly, the proposal called for establishing procedures for the appraisal of management by the board of directors.

Takeovers : Proxy Fights and Tender Offers

While management has long dominated the directors of publicly held corporations, it has more recently become active in taking over other managements and directors. This has been possible because the proxy system, which normally insures the perpetuation of management and its handpicked directors, is a two-edged sword: it can also dethrone any management and board.

In recent years this threat has become a constant presence for many U.S. corporations whose solid assets, poor earnings and low stock price-earnings ratios have made them easy victims of the takeover. Because of antitrust laws and other government regulations, the largest corporations—including nearly all those in the *Fortune* 500—have rarely been targets, but the takeover game built the big conglomerates, and it has also enriched many smaller companies seeking fast growth and quick profits.

Takeovers, whether "friendly" or "unfriendly," are never simple operations. In a friendly one, a small corporation is usually acquired by a larger one which by repeated takeovers may have become a cash-rich conglomerate of unrelated businesses. Management of the smaller company agrees to the merger because it believes management as well as the company will benefit or because it is vulnerable and wants to escape a threatened takeover by unfriendly parties.

An unfriendly takeover may be accomplished in the old-fashioned way by winning a drawn-out fight for the stockholders' votes, but such fights are now rare. One of the classic battles by an individual stockholder was the fierce clash between John D. Rockefeller, Jr., and Col. Robert W. Stewart, board chairman of Standard Oil of Indiana in 1929. Because Stewart became implicated in the Teapot Dome oil scandals, Rockefeller asked him to resign. But Stewart refused, and he had the backing of the entire board and nearly all 25,000 employees, one-third of whom were stockholders.

Rockefeller, who personally owned only 5 percent of the voting stock, spent some $800,000 on letters to stockholders, hiring legal experts and generally promoting his personal stature (and attacking Stewart's) in order to sway stockholders to his side. Stewart claimed he was the victim of "a cowardly and dastardly libel," and at the annual meeting the stockholders—including all but 17 of 7,900 employees—voted for him two to one. But Rockefeller, with the backing of the major stockholders, got 65 percent of the shares voted for his slate of directors, which then banished Stewart. Rockefeller wasn't vindictive; all of Stewart's loyal board members were re-elected except the general counsel—and he was re-appointed to that post.

Far more common today are the unfriendly takeovers in which a "target" or "pigeon" has been hunted down and captured by an ambitious, growth-happy company or by a ruthless operator out to manipulate the company's stock for a capital gain. Such takeovers are achieved by a tempting, shrewdly calculated "tender offer"—an offer to pay, in cash and/or an exchange of stock, a premium price for most or all of the shares "tendered" by stockholders of the target company.

Then those stock market professionals called arbitrageurs often get into the game, buying up big blocks of the target company's stock at prices below the takeover bid and hoping to cash in by helping the raider scare shareholders into selling out. But a defending target company may also use arbitrageurs in getting the raider to raise his bid. In 1977 arbitrageurs were estimated to have some $300 million tied up in an assortment of takeover deals.

In their rush to conglomerate, corporations have had little trouble capturing vulnerable companies by exchanging shares because the stock market usually puts a much higher price on a conglomerate's shares. The exchange of shares provides a sizable tax-free bonus to those who sell out. However, the tender offers for cash, not an exchange of stock, were most responsible for the flood of mergers that rose to more than 5,000 a year during the late 1960s.

The raiding business was already booming when Congress passed the Williams Act in 1968, making cash tender offers reasonably legal and fairly respectable. The act requires raiders to disclose more detailed data about themselves and prohibits secret takeovers by mandating that the raider reveal his plans and disclose his holdings of the target's stock no more than ten days after he acquires more than 5 percent of such stock.

But the raider usually has given the target company's stockholders only seven days to accept his offer—the minimum time required by the Williams Act. It is this time pressure that has made tender offers so tricky, arduous and exhausting for both sides. Often the CEO of a target company first learns of a raider's offer on seeing it proclaimed in a one- or two-page newspaper ad. With only a week to convince stockholders that they should support the present management, the CEO has had to scramble to assemble a battery of specialized talents known as "hired guns" to try to block the takeover.

A team of such specialists in law, banking, proxy solicitation and public relations may work out a variety of defensive tactics. It may (1) find another company (a "white knight") willing to take over on friendly terms (i.e., retaining present management), (2) begin a press campaign to justify management and discredit the raider, (3) initiate reforms in management to answer the raider's charges of incompetence and (4) seek intensively the votes of major stockholders.

Numerous other steps can be taken if a company has sufficient advance warning that it might become a target for a raider. It may then acquire a company that is regulated by the government and cannot be taken over without government approval. The directors may take a number of legal steps that will throw obstacles in the raider's path; the board may (1) authorize the issue of preferred convertible stock to friendly investors, (2) eliminate the bylaw allowing stockholders to call a special meeting of shareholders, (3) change the bylaws to stagger the terms of the directors so the raider can't vote all of them out at once, (4) postpone the annual meeting to provide more time for soliciting proxies and (5) change the company's state of incorporation to gain the protection of state laws that favor the target company.

Since 1968 state legislators have been passing new takeover laws, and by 1977 more than a score of such statutes had lengthened the tender offer period. Many extended it to twenty days or more (in Delaware the raider must notify the state commissioner twenty days before he makes his bid and must then keep his bid open for another twenty days). Some states also now require hearings to insure full disclosure of the raider's plans and to explore the "fairness" of his offer, thereby further delaying matters and giving the target company more chance to escape or beat the offer. State laws can increase takeover costs by one million dollars or more.

The new state laws were abruptly challenged in 1977 when a U.S. court in Dallas ruled that the takeover law in Idaho (the target's home state) was unconstitutional because it interfered with interstate commerce and thwarted the purpose of the 1968 Williams Act by which Congress intended to maintain a fair balance between raiders and target companies. The decision in the case (Great Western United Corp. v. Sunshine Mining Co.) was, not surprisingly, appealed; if upheld, it would surely increase the risks of target companies relying on similar laws in 27 other states—and it would encourage other raiders to challenge such laws and go ahead with their tender offers.

State takeover laws have also been challenged by the SEC which in 1976 presented a proposed set of takeover rules. If adopted, these would take precedence over any state laws with which they might conflict. Among other things, the SEC proposed on the one hand to help a target company by increasing from seven to fifteen days the period in which he might escape or block a raider—plus ten more days if the raider raised his bid; on the other hand, the SEC would help a raider by requiring his target to make available its list of stockholders.

Objections to these proposals came immediately from state officials and from corporate executives, lawyers, bankers and others whose interests they affected directly. Management's self-interest was obvious: If the SEC had its way, takeovers might be easier to accomplish, and while a raider may allow a former CEO to stay on as a director on the raider's new board, other directors and executives, and sometimes everyone in middle management, are usually not even pawns in the takeover games—they end up out in the cold.

Such extreme actions have given raiders a bad name. That

they are now often regarded as "bad guys" only proves how well management has persuaded lawyers, businessmen, judges and most stockholders that any corporate management has a "right" to its power and should not be disturbed. Indeed, the overthrow of an established management is generally regarded today as an undesirable act.

There is no logical basis for such prejudice. The raider is simply using legal machinery to gain his ends, and whatever these may be—lust for power, money, status, perquisites— they are also those of the management he seeks to oust. Moreover, it is a fact that a takeover may greatly benefit a target company by cleaning out managerial deadwood that has barely been keeping the company alive.

Takeovers also directly benefit the legal owners because they enable stockholders to get a much better price for their shares than they could reasonably expect with the old management still in power. And state laws that prolong the tender offer period have consistently produced an even higher price for a stock than the original raider offered because the longer period encouraged other acquisitive companies to bid the price up.

This was dramatically demonstrated in the spring and summer of 1977 when a fierce, three-cornered takeover struggle upset a Wall Street cliché that billion dollar companies are too big to be taken over. After 5 months of tactical and legal maneuvering, Babcock & Wilcox, an engineering firm with over $1.5 billion in sales finally succumbed to the tender offer of J. Ray McDermott Co., an engineering firm with sales of over $1 billion, which had entered the bidding to block the tender offer of United Technologies Corp., an engineering company whose sales were over $5.5 billion. Bidding and counterbidding boosted the price of Babcock &

Wilcox's shares from less than $30 to $62, and the in-fighting involved lawsuits, delaying tactics behind Ohio's takeover law, personality conflicts and strategies of three bands of takeover experts, including the two "top guns" in the business.

This takeover war showed that the directors of large corporations face the same severe test that tender offers present to directors of smaller corporations. They have to protect themselves against charges of failing to discharge their responsibilities by carefully assessing the tender offer. Since a takeover automatically rewards the stockholders, directors may be liable if they help management defeat a raider in order to protect its status as well as their own. They may also be liable if they accept, without investigating its consequences, an offer that delights the stockholders.

For directors today the takeover game poses additional sobering questions. Is the tender offer fair and beneficial to all the company's employees? to its customers? to the local communities involved? to the public interest? A director who decides a tender offer simply in terms of its consequences for the stockholders or for management and the directors themselves, does not yet understand the meaning of fiduciary responsibility.

4

The Invisible Network

Interlocking Directors: The Enduring Web

It is nearly ninety years since the Sherman Anti-Trust Act outlawed combinations in restraint of trade and encouraged the hopes of reformers that the monopolistic power of the big trusts would be broken. Those trusts have indeed disappeared, but the major source of their power—the web of directors that connected banks, insurance companies, corporations and their suppliers and competitors—still operates despite the dominance of management.

Directors who assume that interlocking directorships is a long dead issue have much to learn about the status and role of certain directors. The adroit use of directorships is the same leverage investment bankers have applied since the 1880s, when they first raised the ogre of monopoly in the form of huge trusts.

In spite of the Sherman Act trusts were bigger than ever by the early 1900s. Their critics were stoutly answered by a

Wall Street publisher, John Moody, who revealed in *The Truth About Trusts* facts and statistics concerning a total of 445 corporate combinations, including seven major trusts (steel, copper, smelting, sugar, tobacco, shipping and oil) that embraced 1,500 different plants under the control of Morgan or Rockefeller interests through the device of interlocking directorships. For Moody the trusts deserved the credit for making America a tremendous industrial success.

In 1911 the U.S. Supreme Court held that trusts were legal as long as they did not employ "unreasonable" restraints of trade. The following year the Pujo committee revealed still more about interlocking directorships and their influence over competition, prices and markets. Monopoly again became a hot political issue. Ironically, former president Teddy Roosevelt was no longer a trust buster; he argued only for stricter regulation of the trusts. But presidential candidate Woodrow Wilson campaigned for the "New Freedom," urging that the root causes of the trusts, particularly the interlocking directorships, be abolished so that the United States could again be an economy of freely competitive small enterprisers.

Wilson had adopted the ideas of a crusading Boston lawyer, Louis D. Brandeis, who in 1913 wrote a series of articles attacking big corporations, investment bankers and interlocking directors. *Other People's Money and How the Bankers Use It* charged that interlocking directorships were "the root of many evils," including suppression of competition, violation of the Sherman Act, disloyalty and inefficiency. The practice, he said, substituted "the pull of privilege for the push of manhood."

As an example of "the endless chain" of control, Brandeis described how the Morgan oligarchy could influence, through interlocking directorships, the New Haven railroad, Guaranty Trust Co., Penn Mutual Life Insurance Co., U.S. Steel, General Electric, Western Union, AT&T, the Reading railroad, the Pullman Co. and the Baldwin Locomotive Co.

The arguments of Brandeis and others helped to pass the Clayton Act in 1914, a law that ostensibly outlawed interlocking directorships. But the courts equivocated on the meaning of the law and continued to sanction such directorships for nonfinancial corporations. Brandeis, elevated to the Supreme Court, returned to the attack in the 1920s and again in the 1930s. He republished *Other People's Money* in 1935, arguing that the NRA had proved how inefficient big corporations were.

Since then the issue of interlocking directorships has faded from view, but the practice continues to be pervasive. A study by Professor Peter C. Dooley in 1965 showed that 233 of the 250 largest corporations were interlocked by mutual directors; thirty years before, the figure had been 225 of the 250 largest companies. Banks were found to be interlocked nearly twice as often as industrial corporations, and the number of interlocks between banks and their corporate customers increased as the latter became less solvent.

The Dooley study identified "local interest groups" in fifteen major U.S. cities to which nearly half the 250 corporations belonged. Banks and life insurance companies were the core of all these local groups. In the New York group of 38 large organizations, six banks interlocked 95 times, 4 insurance companies interlocked 72 times, and each of 24 big corporations interlocked 10 or more times with others in the group.

"The institution of the interlocking directorate," as Dooley put it, "is extensive and enduring." His findings tended to prove that big corporations are not nearly so independent and self-sufficient as economists and others have claimed. He concluded that the presence of financiers, local business leaders and competitors on a board was a constraining influence on management—and he found that corporations with the most inside directors had the least interlocks.

Yet the influence of even one financier-director is not to be underestimated, particularly when management is borrowing from his bank. And the web of banker directorships is becoming ever more significant as the size of corporate pension funds grows and billions of employees' dollars are invested, through bankers, in the stocks of other large corporations. Banks may one day hold so much proxy control of corporations that the longstanding question of interlocking directorates could again become the serious concern of Congress, the courts and the public.

The Silent, Hidden Accomplices

One of the best kept secrets of the large corporation is the identity and potential leverage of those who are known as the "proprietary" owners of its stock. These are the nonhuman owners, those institutions that, like brokers, buy, hold and sell stock on behalf of corporate and individual customers. They include pension funds, mutual funds, trust funds, money-management funds and the holdings of foundations and insurance and religious organizations.

These institutional stock holdings add up to enormous sums; they are estimated to total more than one trillion dollars. Nearly two-thirds of this is said to be held by banks —and bankers have traditionally become directors of corporations that borrow heavily from them and give them their pension funds to manage.

The influence of bankers on the boards of large corporations has tremendous potential. Some 50 commercial banks in the United States, it has been reported, held more than 5 percent of the voting stock of 145 of the 500 largest corporations in 1967 and had 768 interlocking directorates with 268 of the largest corporations. One bank alone, Morgan Guaranty Trust of New York, whose trust department is the largest in the United States, in 1972 held 5 percent or more of the common stock of 72 major corporations and had representatives on more than 100 corporate boards.

The identities of those empowered to vote the vast bank holdings of corporate stock remain carefully hidden by the universal refusal of bankers to divulge the actual or "beneficial" ownership of their trust accounts. And there are similarly unidentified millions of shares held by insurance companies and investment and brokerage houses that, like the banks, use "nominee" and "street" names—pseudonyms that cover their identities as the proprietary owners. Some of these identities have been revealed by Senator Lee Metcalf and others who have investigated the institutional control of corporations. Some use many names; Prudential Insurance Co., for example, has used a string of names such as Aftco, Cadco, Quinco, etc. Other names that mask large holdings are Kane & Co. and Cudd & Co. (Chase Manhattan Bank, N.A.); Carson & Co., Powers & Co. and Tegge & Co. (Morgan Guaranty Trust Co.); and Cede & Co. (Depository Trust Co., a subsidiary of the New York Stock Exchange). This last company was revealed by Senator Metcalf in 1972 to have been the largest stockholder in 36 of 132 corporations that responded to his inquiries, and it held more than 10 percent of the shares of 16 of those companies.

While the proprietary owners of voting stock are supposed to vote their holdings according to the wishes of their clients, proxy forms, special rules and the indifference of the beneficial owners leave the decisions almost entirely in the hands of the institutional holders—who commonly support management. In Senator Metcalf's words, "institutions as a group have a record of voting involvement that displays relatively little opposition to management."

However, in recent years a few universities and foundations have been moved to vote their institutional holdings against management and in support of causes and campaigns in the public interest. Such issues as the Arab-Israel conflict and South African apartheid have on occasion changed the voting habits of some large institutional stockholders. Until they are persuaded or pressed to do otherwise, however, these stockholders can be expected to remain the hidden accomplices of management, silently abdicating their voting rights under cover of the blank-check proxy system.

Congress in 1975 considered but failed to pass laws covering the concentration of stock ownership under nominee and street names, and both the SEC and the American Society of Corporate Secretaries investigated the practice through questionnaires in 1976. The SEC found that the practice had more benefits (mostly in facilitating stock transfers) than disadvantages, including the masking of "beneficial ownership" that has complicated the SEC's work on disclosure. However, the SEC now has the power to require institutional investors to report the identities and holdings of clients owning more than 5 percent of any security.

Managements are also greatly interested in knowing who their biggest stockholders are, and they would like to have a system that would give them that information. But bankers, brokers and many large stockholders oppose the idea as an invasion of their right to privacy and a disruption of the present system that would impose heavy costs and record-keeping requirements. Such opposition will undoubtedly continue until Congress settles it with specific, detailed legislation.

5

Running the Risks

The Liability Puzzle

Liability has become a scare word for directors of large, publicly held corporations. And they have a right to be alarmed. In recent years decisions by the courts and the SEC have not only widened the scope of directors' liability but so complicated it that even experienced lawyers cannot be sure just what risks directors are running.

Directors are themselves mostly to blame for their present anxious state. Their fears would be relatively small had they not been so complacent about their responsibilities and allowed management to assume their basic functions. Aiding and abetting the complacency of directors, the courts until recently have been extremely lenient in their treatment of negligent directors. Unwilling to question the "business judgment" of directors, judges have rarely fined—and never jailed—directors who failed to question management's behavior or who profited personally as insiders serving two or three masters.

A good deal of the difficulty in defining a director's liability lies in the vague and disputable meanings attributed to the role. Courts have repeatedly declared that a director is not legally a "trustee" to be held to strict accountability but a "fiduciary" with the twin duties of diligence and loyalty. In common law a director is expected to be, on the one hand, careful and prudent in carrying out his duties under state statutes and corporation bylaws and, on the other hand, loyal to the corporation without profiting personally from business opportunities that belong to the corporation, having a conflict of interest in serving the corporation or acting to compete with the corporation.

Beyond these standards some courts have set much higher ones. A fiduciary, one judge held, "must act in accordance with the highest standards which a man of the finest honor might impose upon himself." As Justice Benjamin Cardozo so elegantly phrased it in 1928, he must have "not honesty alone, but the punctilio of an honor the most sensitive."

Few directors are that sensitive today. The great majority, however, are honest men who want to act within the law and who expect the managements of their coporations to do the same. Since the moral values of directors vary considerably, however, what is honor for one may be impractical idealism for another. Thus directors rely on their lawyers to guide them through the maze of legal decisions and SEC opinions that now surrounds the definition of their liability.

It is naive to assume that directors can always operate within the law; the laws and the regulations are too numerous and too unclear in too many situations. Some landmark decisions in recent years have widened—and some have narrowed—the spectrum of directors' liability. In the SEC's case against Texas Gulf Sulphur in 1968, for example, the court clarified some points about insider trading on inside information and the disclosure of facts, but the court also expressed concern about many related but unanswered questions.

Another notable case, *Escott* v. *BarChris Construction Co.,* established clearly in 1969 the liability of directors who fail to exercise "due diligence" and instead rely on management and other experts for the information disclosed in registration statements without making "reasonable" investigations on their own. But court decisions since then have continued to amplify and specify those areas where directors had better be prudent in verifying the actions and statements of management and its advisors.

Directors on bank boards have lately been jolted on learning of suits brought by the Federal Deposit Insurance Corporation against directors of failed banks. Heavy losses in real estate loans have been largely responsible for the rise in bank failures from an average of five a year in 1970–74 to about 15 a year in 1975 and 1976. The FDIC had more than a dozen cases pending in 1977 against directors charged with "willful negligence." In its case against a bank in Chattanooga, whose failure was the third largest in U.S. history, the FDIC said the directors were "personally and collectively" liable for $12 million lost in bad loans because they failed to use "due diligence" in discovering management's unsafe lending practices. Although the FDIC has settled such cases for a fraction of the losses, directors have to face the grim fact that liability insurance does not protect them in cases of "willful negligence."

What further complicates the liability puzzle for directors is the steady expansion of their responsibilities as seen by employees, consumers, communities and the federal government—as well as by stockholders. Deceiving investors, bribing politicians, misusing assets and polluting the environment are now major liabilities for directors, and many other corporate acts, such as pirating employees, closing down plants and making unsafe products, are likely to bring charges against directors who fail to do their duty diligently. It seems clear that a director must accept his responsibility as a fiduciary who represents the interests of many groups, some of which are in direct conflict with others.

What Is "Disclosure"?

Any director who tries to learn the extent of his liabilities will soon run across that crucial word "disclosure." This is the term that puts the bite into the federal securities laws while being notably absent from most state laws. In broad terms, disclosure means that corporations with more than one million dollars in assets and whose securities are publicly listed are legally bound under the Securities Acts of 1933 and 1934 to report to the SEC everything about their operations and personnel that might affect investors' decisions to buy, hold or sell their securities.

Disclosure must be prompt (delays might be misleading), public (otherwise it's a form of "tipping" information to insiders) and full and accurate (omitted or erroneous facts could deceive investors). This applies to everything disclosed in registration statements, prospectuses for new issues, current, quarterly and annual reports, proxy materials, tender offers, press releases and the stock trading of directors, officers and other insiders privy to a corporation's strategies and decisions.

Of all the situations in which a director is likely to become

liable for nondisclosure, these are the most hazardous:
- Self dealing—especially profiting from inside informa-
  tion in stock transactions
- Acquisitions and takeover bids
- Fraudulent management
- Companies with high price-earnings ratios subject to
  manipulation with accounting devices
- Companies dominated by a chief executive who with-
  holds information from the board

The risks of disclosure have been vastly complicated by a
continuing stream of legal interpretations. While the securities laws specify half a dozen or so major areas of liability for
the director, the SEC, the courts and private legal opinions
have steadily elaborated on the meanings of the terms involved in proving liability. These interpretations, definitions
and implications have become so critical that a director can
never presume to know what they might mean in a particular
case. Nor can he expect to become an expert in all the legal
niceties. But at least he can be aware of what the basic terms
may mean for him in trying to discharge his obligations as
a director.

Materiality is critical in determining liability for nondisclosure; it refers to the significance or importance of facts
that should be disclosed. The concept was carefully described by the Supreme Court in a 1976 decision that stated
that an omitted fact is "material" if there is "a substantial
likelihood" that a reasonable shareholder would consider it
important in deciding how to vote in a proxy case. The Court
said this standard of materiality does not require proof that
disclosure of the fact would have caused the investor to
change his vote; the fact need only assume "actual signifi-

cance" in his deliberations or be viewed as having "significantly altered the 'total mix.' "

In other cases the meaning of materiality may be judged to be broader. An SEC report on illegal payments, for example, indicated that the term may have been widened to include matters relating to "the integrity of management." It is notable that RCA's directors withdrew a registration statement and asked for the resignation of the CEO as soon as they learned he had failed to disclose the fact that he hadn't filed income tax returns for five years—conduct which they found "inappropriate for a man in his position." Auditors, on the other hand, tend to regard as not material some facts that the SEC's lawyers firmly believe should be disclosed.

Scienter is another yardstick term over which lawyers, courts and the SEC tangle; it can be defined as a state of mind involving intent to defraud. It applies to a director who knows a matter is other than it is represented to be, or isn't sure whether it is so or has an "evil motive" in not disclosing it. In 1976 the Supreme Court held that "scienter" was necessary to prove liability in private suits brought under SEC rule 10b-5 (disclosures connected with stock transactions). But apparently it did not apply to suits involving misleading proxy statements. Such uncertainties, shifting from case to case, continue to abound.

The business judgment rule has been described by the courts in different ways; essentially it refers to the exercise of discretion or judgment by directors and officers who have acted "in good faith" for the benefit of the corporation. The timing of a disclosure, for example, has been held a valid matter for business judgment to decide. The withholding of information may also, in management's judgment, be held to serve a valid corporate purpose. The courts have long given directors and officers wide latitude under this rule, but their tolerance now appears to be waning.

Duty of care describes a director's diligence in keeping informed about the corporation and its management; it is his obligation to inquire into what is going on in the company. State statutes generally recommend "diligence," "care" and "skill" for directors (the Delaware act is silent about the duty of care, leaving this to the courts). A recent definition in the Model Business Corporation Act says a director should serve "in good faith, in a manner he reasonably believes to be in the best interests of the corporation, and with such care as an ordinarily prudent person in a like position would use under similar circumstances." The Securities Act of 1933 established a duty of diligence, or "due diligence," by stating that a director can protect himself from liability for false registration statements by showing that "after reasonable investigation" he believed the statements were true, were not misleading and omitted no material fact.

The "right to rely"—the right of directors to depend on management for information, reports, statements and opinions—has been spelled out in varying detail. Generally, it means that a director can rely on information provided by officers, lawyers, bankers, accountants, appraisers, consultants and board committees *if* the director "reasonably believes" them to be reliable and competent. But if he has information that makes him doubt the reliability of such sources, he is likely to be held liable if he acts on their data or advice.

The SEC: Expanding Watchdog

In considering his liabilities, the average timid director can expect to remain confused by the intricacies of court decisions and the maze of overlapping and interlocking federal regulations. But at least some of his confusion would disappear if he understood better the role of the Securities and Exchange Commission and what has happened to it since the Watergate scandals of 1972–1974.

A brainchild of President Franklin D. Roosevelt, the SEC was created by the Securities Exchange Act of 1934. It was set up as a watchdog not of the nation's corporations but of the securities markets and with a strong emphasis on "disclosure." Congress assumed that because securities frauds and stock manipulations are nearly always carried out with the cooperation of the companies involved, those activities would be curbed by requiring corporations to disclose to investors full and accurate information about themselves.

During the next six years the SEC was given the administration of four other laws regulating securities and finance in addition to the Securities Act of 1933, which had made directors liable for false registration statements.* The SEC also became advisor to the federal courts in corporate reorganization proceedings under Chapter X of the National Bankruptcy Act.

The SEC was partly shielded from political pressures by being made a bipartisan, independent, quasi-judicial agency of the government. No more than three of its five commissioners may belong to the same political party, and, with the advice and counsel of the Senate, they are appointed by the President. They serve five-year terms which are staggered so that one expires each year on June 5. The President also designates the chairman, whose term may be brief (between

*The Public Utilities Holding Company Act of 1935, the Trust Indenture Act of 1939, the Investment Company Act of 1940 and the Investment Advisors Act of 1940.

1972 and 1975 three of the chairmen appointed by President
Nixon resigned).

By 1977 the SEC's staff had grown to some 2,000 employees, including lawyers, accountants, security analysts,
examiners, administrators and clerks. The five operating
divisions in Washington devise policies for the commissioners' approval and handle specific functions: enforcement
(securities laws), market regulation (stock exchanges and
brokers), corporation finance (filed statements, tender offers,
stockholder resolutions, etc.), corporate regulations (utility
holding companies) and investment management (mutual
funds and investment advisors). Each of the nine regional
administrators is appointed by the commission, which makes
an annual report to Congress.

Until 1974 few directors worried about the disclosure rules
of the SEC. But in that year a newly appointed head of the
enforcement division, a tough, aggressive lawyer named
Stanley Sporkin, put his staff on the trail of a score of corporations whose managements had admitted to the Watergate
prosecutor that they had made illegal payments from secret
"slush funds" to the Committee to Re-elect the President.

The confessions woke the SEC up to the fact that its forty
years of policing corporate securities had failed to reveal
these illegal payments and that countless other companies
must have set up slush funds they hadn't disclosed. Knowing
that his staff of fewer than 200 could never investigate them
all, Sporkin asked all publicly held corporations to investigate themselves "voluntarily" and to report to the SEC what
they found. The SEC said it would sue any corporation that
refused to do this and would have the courts order a separate
investigation by outside auditors and directors approved by
the SEC.

By 1977 this "voluntary" program had involved more than 350 companies and over a score of enforcement actions. Many of the biggest and best known corporations confessed to bribes, payoffs and kickbacks totaling millions of dollars. In several cases chief executives, board chairmen and senior executives were fired or resigned when their directors learned they had been hoodwinked by management. Other companies in settling stockholder suits agreed to add more outside directors to their boards.

SEC investigations have expanded to uncover commercial as well as political bribery, and some companies have been forced to disclose secret payments that did not in fact violate U.S. laws. In ferreting out what he has called a "corruption of the [capitalistic] process," Sporkin became convinced that "managers are running corporations like piggy banks" and "have taken upon themselves to do anything they damn well please with corporations."

After 21 months of treating leniently corporations that confessed, the SEC terminated its program of voluntary disclosure in 1977. The commission had not promised immunity from prosecution, but the likelihood of legal action was definitely reduced. The rationale for the program seemed to be that if a corporation didn't volunteer disclosure, it would risk an SEC investigation that could expose "all the gory details"—including names and amounts. These would show that the company hadn't been able or willing to prevent the fraud, and it would be customary for the court to ask for an accounting.

The SEC has backed up its tough attitude toward corporate hanky-panky with legal action in recent years. In 1975, for example, it ordered 153 injunctive actions, referred 88 criminal reference reports to the Justice Department and got

116 convictions in 33 cases while 10 of 17 defendants in criminal contempt cases were also convicted.

The disclosures of illegal funds and payments have inevitably alerted two other government agencies. The Internal Revenue Service wants to know whether the secret payments were hidden in tax returns as business expenses, and the Federal Trade Commission could also query whether the use of such payments may result in unfair competition under the antitrust laws. A Justice Department task force has been set up to press criminal charges under other laws.

Corporations sued by the SEC risk contempt proceedings if they continue to make undisclosed payments. Even so, a few companies have informed the SEC that they intend to continue the practice when, in their opinion, a situation leaves them no alternative. Only congressional legislation seems likely to settle the touchy issue of corporate kickbacks and bribery. Meanwhile the SEC, having no mandate to police the ethics of the nation's 25,000 publicly held corporations, is using its post-Watergate tactics to enforce its ethics —as well as the law—on the 9,600 or so companies that report to it.

Early in 1977 the commission, reversing an earlier decision, proposed that the identity of any officer or director involved in making questionable corporate payments should be disclosed in proxy statements. And the commission took a dim view of corporate policy statements regarding such payments, which, it said, are "subject to public relations posturing or to the recitation of boiler-plate assertions of good faith, and do not permit any type of verification."

Furthermore, since 1976 the SEC has proposed other amendments to the securities laws that would greatly enlarge its watchdog role. One set of proposals asked corporations to disclose to investors the "backgrounds" of management, including such information about its "qualification, remuneration and transactions" as is now required in the annual 10-K reports filed with the commission. Directors would be required to reveal what board committees they served on, what directorships they held in other companies, and any "material events" in their backgrounds, such as legal injunctions and convictions within the previous five years.

The commission has also proposed to develop a standard by which all forms of top management compensation might be easily compared. Officers and directors would be asked to disclose "all forms of remuneration" they received, including salaries, bonuses, fees, and personal benefits known as perquisites. They could exclude any "incidental" or fringe benefits directly related to their jobs, such as reserved parking places and business lunches; but they would be expected to report the dollar values of a host of other fringe benefits ranging from home repairs and living and vacation expenses to automobiles, yachts, club memberships and favorable loans.

These proposals raised such a storm of questions that the SEC issued a detailed "interpretation" to clarify the distinctions it proposed to make between job-related benefits and personal benefits. But the interpretations only intensified the questioning; even the SEC's attorneys were stymied by the complexity of the queries they received.

Clearly in 1977 the SEC was showing a new inclination to get corporations to divulge more and more information to investors and shareholders. Hearings were scheduled to begin on a wide range of subjects concerning "corporate governance" which had been developed from replies the commission had solicited from investors and other interested parties. The commission aimed to explore and discuss corporate behavior in all these areas: environmental and equal employment matters; shareholder proposals; shareholder access to management's proxy materials used in nominating directors; increased disclosure of the qualifications of those nominated to a board; a review of the proxy procedures used by institutional investors and whether they should be required, before voting such shares, to secure the views of those who owned the shares.

Whatever comes of these and other proposals under the commission's new chairman, Harold M. Williams, the SEC seems likely to be considerably more alert as a watchdog than it has been under previous commissioners.

SEC Guidelines: A Balancing Act

Every director has good reason to be apprehensive about the rules of the one federal agency that has regulating power over those things that usually get directors into trouble. SEC regulations cover a lot of ground and require, among other things, compliance with rules concerning proxies, elections of directors, fraud in trading, sale of control, insider trading, stockholder proposals and full disclosure of material facts to present and prospective investors.

Presumably, too, the SEC is in the best position to establish guidelines that would let directors know specifically what standards should be followed to avoid being held liable for negligence or fraud. In 1973 SEC Chairman G. Bradford Cook directed the commission staff to prepare guidelines for directors, and when Cook moved on, his successor, Ray Garrett, took over the assignment.

In May 1974, however, Garrett had to confess that there would be no SEC guidelines. In a talk to the Conference Board he explained to that business research organization why the staff could not agree on a set of guidelines. The task of trying to set standards for many different kinds of directors was one complication: Garrett questioned whether the same standards should apply to inside directors, outside directors and specialized directors (bankers, accountants, scientists) and whether the standards governing decisions on major transactions (such as mergers) should be stiffer than those concerning routine business matters.

Garrett also cited a number of steps a director might take should he suspect fraud: he could discuss the problem and ask for a vote on it; he could resign; or he could report it to the authorities, to the press, to the stockholders or to other principals involved. But as Garrett pointed out, reporting a fraud doubles the risks for a director. If he is wrong in his allegations, the company could sue him for slander; if he is right, either the SEC or a third party principal to the deal could sue him for having done nothing when he knew a fraud was about to occur.

Protecting directors, however, has never been a prime concern of the SEC. Its characteristic attitude, reflecting that of Congress, is a kind of balancing act between conflicting interests. In amending the Securities Acts in 1975 Congress emphasized the need to protect the privacy of investors by providing that the disclosure of information about personal accounts need not be required. So the SEC has held that the securities laws "must be carefully balanced against the need to assure the protection of individual rights to privacy in personal financial dealings," while at the same time protecting the interests of investors.

This balancing act has consistently confused and complicated both the SEC's proposed amendments to its rules and those it has finally adopted. The confusions have become glaring in the commission's grappling with the intricacies of corporate takeovers. Congress ruled in the Williams Act that "takeover bids should not be discouraged," but also said there should be "full and fair disclosure for the benefit of investors" without at the same time "tipping the balance" either in favor of management or of those making the takeover bid.

In 1975 after an investigation and hearings lasting several months the SEC proposed that corporations disclose specific information regarding takeovers and those "beneficial owners" who possess more than 5 percent of a corporation's voting stock. It defined such owners as those who can vote or dispose of the shares, or receive dividends or proceeds from the sale of the securities. The SEC also proposed that corporations reveal the identities and holdings of the 30 largest stockholders* and information about those controlling the ten largest blocks of stock. And in 1976 other proposals were advanced, including one that would for the first time allow a raider access to a target company's list of shareholders so they could be solicited by mail, and another that would require tender offers to stay open for at least 15 days.

Like all SEC proposals, however, these had to endure a long and tortuous process of amending, expanding, appending, obscuring and deleting their original meanings. Pressures for such changes come from corporations, lawyers,

---

*According to evidence given to a congressional subcommittee in 1972, the 30 biggest stockholders held 41 percent of Chrysler's voting stock, 35 percent of Ford's and 28 percent of Mobil's.

bankers, brokers, trustees, trade groups, state agencies and other "interested parties." Thus early in 1977 on the basis of 225 letters from such sources the SEC changed its definition of "beneficial owner" (the reference to receiving dividends was dropped, for example) and it withdrew completely its proposal covering the disclosure of the 30 largest stockholders and those controlling the ten largest blocks of stock. A variety of complaints about the last two proposals had convinced the SEC that they would not provide "material" information to investors, would be "unnecessarily burdensome" to those reporting, might be "an unwarranted invasion of privacy," would be "neither legally nor logistically feasible," and "could be utilized in takeover attempts to give the offeror an advantage not presently available and not intended by Congress."

Whatever guidelines the SEC has to offer obviously have to be dug out of the ponderous, nit-picking legalese in which its proposals, amendments and rules are embedded. One 1977 release on "Beneficial Ownership Disclosure Requirements," for example, ran to more than 20,000 words. The process of drafting proposals, soliciting the views of "interested parties," holding hearings, digesting comments, revising drafts, getting new objections and taking "final action" can consume years. So many additional questions about "beneficial ownership" had been raised by mid-1977, for example, that the SEC decided to postpone the effective date of its rulings for eight months, to April 1978.

Yet after a 17-month study of the SEC's disclosure system, an advisory panel reported in 1977 that the system was working all right and needed only minor changes. The panel made no recommendations on the sensitive subject of disclosing illegal corporate actions because, according to its chairman, former Commissioner Sommer, this would add "one more voice to an already fevered-pitch debate." Nor did the panel propose any clarification of the issue of "materiality" that might indicate which acts were important and which were not. Such distinctions are what lawyers especially would like to have; but as others have pointed out, distinctions usually only serve to reveal to lawyers the loopholes through which their clients might escape liability and prosecution.

It is possible that the SEC's hesitant approach to its tasks of regulation may change under its new chairman, Harold M. Williams, who took over in August 1977. Williams had been a tax lawyer, a top executive and board chairman of a big conglomerate (Norton Simon Inc.) before he resigned in 1970 to head UCLA's business school. Having served on an SEC advisory panel and on the boards of four corporations, he is aware of the problems of both.

Directors, however, cannot expect much sympathy from the new commissioner. While he favors the election of more outside directors and the use of audit committees to control management, he thinks that directors are largely responsible for the poor image of business and for the illegal behavior of corporate managers. And he has harshly blamed those executives he calls the "gutless wonders" who have refused to criticize publicly the immoral behavior of their peers.

Such observations are not to be taken lightly when they come from an experienced and successful businessman. Certainly they are a far cry from the words of former Commissioner Ray Garrett who, refusing to take "a hard line" on SEC's control of corporate conduct, said, "We do not want to make the game so hazardous that no one will play." His logic will escape those directors who, like lawyers, believe that specific guidelines are precisely what is needed to make the game less hazardous. Some directors, however, may hope that the SEC under its new commissioner will shift its balancing act so as to restore the rights of those ultimately responsible for the management of large publicly held corporations.

Protection by Subcommittee

Because a board of directors is essentially a committee, it is usually much too big, too awkward and too slow to perform well. (As the saying goes, a camel is a horse designed by a committee.) But because a board of directors is a committee designed by lawyers who are often politicians, it has the power under state corporation law to protect itself. And this is now accomplished by appointing subcommittees of the board.

The bigger a corporation, the more subcommittees it is likely to have. Most of the pressure for more committees now comes from the directors themselves; they see committees as an easy way to find out more information about a corporation than management may be willing to supply the board. The urge to become better informed is relatively new and has been intensified by the increase in liability risks that directors now face. A good committee—one whose chairman is expert in the committee's area—can help protect the rest of the board.

The executive and finance committees have traditionally been expected to warn directors of their responsibilities under state and federal laws. While three out of four large corporations have executive committees, only one in four has a finance committee, and there is some pressure now to combine them, since their memberships often overlap.

These two committees still carry the highest prestige among directors, but three others have been gaining popularity. The compensation committee, which deals with executive salaries and bonuses, is now as prevalent among large corporations as the executive committee. The committee on pensions and stock options ranks third in popularity. But the committee that seems to be multiplying fastest today is the audit committee of the board, now found in about half of the large corporations. As yet no law requires the presence of a committee to oversee the financial statements of a corporation, but audit committees are now firmly recommended by the SEC and the Institute of Certified Public Accountants. And on June 30, 1978, audit committees will be required for all corporations listed on the New York Stock Exchange.

Still other board committees involve directors in a wide variety of problems and issues; each usually includes a "job description" to make certain it does not conflict with management's authority. There are committees on operations, public issues, technology and science, management development, contributions, real estate, building management, mergers, conflicts of interest, shareholder relations, corporate responsibility, management succession, budget, research and development, personal and human resources, and nomination of directors.

From management's viewpoint, committees of the board are most welcome. They give directors the illusion of being put to work without their actually interfering with management control and policies. Another illusion is provided by a committee on compensation, pensions and stock options; it gives the appearance that management is sharing with the board the handling of compensation plans. The virtue of such an appearance was underscored by the specific requirement of the recent legislation on pensions known as ERISA (Employee Retirement Income Security Act) that holds both directors *and* management responsible for the corporation's performance.

From the director's viewpoint a board committee has both advantages and disadvantages. It can dig deeper into matters than a full board can, thereby increasing the board's total output; it gives the board flexibility to act quickly when necessary, as during a threat of takeover; and committees should improve the objectivity of directors in appraising management.

At the same time, however, there are some distinct disadvantages of subcommittees. One, already noted, is the possibility that in searching out more information the committee can increase the liability risks of the full board. Another is that directors often become jealous of those assigned to prestigious committees, and soon all committees become overcrowded. And the more committees a board establishes, the more the nonmembers of the committees will tend to ignore their homework and leave it to the committee to tell them what to do.

The work of the committee completed, there is always the considerable chance that its conclusions and recommendations will be altered or overruled by a dominant CEO. Nevertheless, if a committee's members work hard, their facts and recommendations may do much to restrain an overbearing management and may even detect a useless or a fraudulent one.

6

The Compensation Game

Compensation: Three Hard Facts

A director who serves on a compensation committee of the board soons learns that he faces three hard realities.

The first is that for management—and especially for top executives—the name of the game is unquestionably money. Any director who thinks that "challenges," "opportunities" and "more responsibility" are the prime motivators of management is simply deceiving himself. The desires for security, for perquisites and privileges and for other forms of executive coddling are strong, of course, but as second choices they don't come close to the desire for money. However it may be paid—in salaries, bonuses, pensions, deferred compensation, stock options, "performance" shares, "surrender" shares or credits or "units"—money, by one name or another, is all that management wants most.

The second hard fact is that unless he is a very large stockholder, a director can have no real influence in changing or adjusting the compensation program as developed under the direction of the CEO. Though any CEO should know that he cannot legally, as a director or as an employee, establish his own compensation, nearly all CEOs feel that they are the ones to determine how they and their subordinates should be rewarded.

Usually the CEO supports this delusion by hiring accountants, consultants and so-called compensation experts to develop complex plans covering salaries, bonuses, stock options, retirement pensions and all other fringe benefits. Such plans are said to help "recruit, retain and motivate" the executive team—a claim that has become as untouchable as motherhood, the flag and God. "We know this claim can't be proved," one CEO admitted frankly, "but it is convincing to directors and compensation committees, so why should we give it up until we have something at least as good?"

These plans, worked out under the direction of the CEO, throttle the compensation committee. Very few directors know enough to judge them or have the time to study or question them intelligently. The endless complications concocted by tax laws, tax lawyers, accountants and compensation specialists are more than enough to prevent any director from becoming an "expert" on his own. In fact there are no experts in this area.

The third reality facing the director who sits on a compensation committee is that it is practically impossible to determine rationally what and how corporate executives should be paid. Yet this is the responsibility solely of the directors, according to corporate bylaws and board resolutions, because paying management is obviously not management's job. That would be self-dealing, and, though convictions are rare, the courts have not taken kindly to corporate executives who have been found guilty of rewarding themselves.

The compensation committee, for its part, is in no position to judge management's total performance or to know all the details that affect such performance. The best it can hope to do is to confine its recommendations to the compensation of the CEO (who is at least under the directors' periodic observation) and the other officers elected by the board, usually the treasurer and secretary, whose works are also more or less visible to the board. Compensation for the other members of management has to be left to the CEO and his "experts"—unless the board has the courage to establish a real appraisal program.

Compensation committees are almost never able to do what they are expected to do. Year after year directors continue to allow the chief executive to work out compensation plans for their approval. And any director who questions this procedure can expect the CEO to charge him with "interfering with my authority." The charge is nonsense—no CEO has such authority—but because of this management attitude, directors assigned to compensation committees may reasonably assume that they are low men on the board's totem pole.

The Tip of the Iceberg

Any experienced director knows that there is little rhyme or reason in the executive compensation programs of large corporations. But few directors are concerned enough to question how the CEO and his compensation "experts" arrive at the pay scales they recommend to the board or to the compensation committee.

This attitude was perhaps excusable prior to World War II, when management compensation was relatively simple. About two-thirds of a CEO's total compensation then was usually in salary, the rest in bonus and pension payments. But in the 1950s a host of changes occurred; stock options, deferred compensation deals and other "incentive" programs made their appearance, and total executive compensation suddenly soared to a new and permanently high plateau. One survey showed that it would have taken about eight times as much money in salary and bonus as a CEO received in 1940 to equal all that he got in 1963. It would take even more than that today.

Because compensation became such a hot subject for management, the first compensation service was established in the 1950s by the American Management Association. It provided large corporations with a yardstick by which they might measure their executive pay scales and thereby keep them in line with what their competitors were paying. There is, however, little evidence that this or any other yardstick has actually been employed by boards of directors.

The variety and range of salaries and bonuses paid to CEOs and other top officers remain totally unpredictable—and, superficially at least, illogical. Why, for example, should General Motors, with a $1.2 billion profit in 1975, have paid its chairman a salary of $300,000 and a bonus of $240,000, while Ford Motor Co., with one-sixth of GM's profits in 1975, paid both its chairman and its president $334,000 and no bonus? Why, among the fifteen highest-paid executives that year, should the man who ranked tenth have received the highest salary ($492,000) and the lowest bonus ($111,-000)? Why should the biggest bonus ($550,000) have gone to the chairman of a conglomerate, Rapid-American Corp., which showed that year a net loss of $9 million?

If the answers to these and similar questions are known, they are not likely to be divulged by the directors or executives involved. One analysis has shown that the most important factor in determining compensation is the personality of the CEO: generally speaking, the more dominant the CEO, the higher the rewards. A corporation's size is next in importance, but sales volume, business results and the kind of compensation system used generally account only for minor variations in total compensation.

Directors, in any case, rarely have anything to do with determining the CEO's salary and bonus. The figures are generally presented to the board or the committee by a director who has been told privately what it will take to keep the CEO happy in his work. Those amounts roughly determine what his subordinates will receive; the No. 2 man usually gets about 75 percent of what the CEO receives in salary and bonus, the No. 3 man about 60 percent, and the fourth and fifth level executives successively less. If the CEO holds both the board chairmanship and the presidency, the No. 2 man will generally get less, averaging only about two-thirds of the top salary and bonus. But if these positions are held by different executives, the No. 2 man will receive close to 80 percent of the CEO's compensation.

The disparities in executive compensation increase enormously when the "incentive" elements are added to the package. Stock option grants remain popular despite the uncertainties of the market, but newer schemes offer fat bonuses with little or no risk. Performance shares, contingent stock credits, "surrender" options and incentive "units" and "credits" can be richly rewarding. The chairman of Continental Oil in 1975 surrendered options in return for stock worth over $2 million—nearly five times his salary that year.

Salaries have long since become a minor part of total executive compensation; in some cases they are only the tip of the iceberg. The chairman of General Dynamics in 1975 was paid $225,000 in salary and $175,000 in bonus; in addition he exercised options on 100,000 shares that gave him a net paper gain of $2.1 million, making his salary less than 10 percent of his total compensation. And undoubtedly this was not the full measure of this CEO's rewards. For over and above salaries, bonuses and incentive compensation executives are now accustomed to receiving an extraordinary number of other fringe benefits—plus a long, long list of perquisites.

Fringes and Perks

A director soon learns that corporate officers expect more— often very much more—than money in payment for their services. Whatever these extras are called—fringe benefits, perquisites or prerogatives*—they are far more varied and numerous than even most executives realize. In addition to such familiar, time-honored benefits as the use of company cars and reserved parking spaces, there are many other "perks," including some that are known only to a few chief executives (rent-free housing, for example, and double pay for vacation time).

Management's interest in extras of all kinds intensified in

---

*These terms are commonly used so loosely that individual definitions have become blurred. All have been applied to nonfinancial benefits awarded (or claimed) in recognition of status, influence or authority, and all may describe benefits as diverse as club memberships and first class air travel.

recent years as tax laws stiffened and executives sought to improve their lifestyles with indirect payments that were taxed lightly or not at all. Since generous extras may be valued more highly than hard cash, corporations have found them useful in recruiting new executives and retaining those who become restless. And since such rewards can be easily buried in the expense figures, CEOs usually have no trouble in getting directors to approve them.

Surveys have revealed the extraordinary variety of extras that management has secured as part of its indirect compensation. A study by *Dun's Review* in 1973 listed 33 such items on a "laundry list" of "indirect pay," and another survey by the American Management Association in 1975, covering 667 companies, showed about the same number of extras. But the two lists were by no means identical, and certainly neither was all-inclusive.

Generally speaking, the bigger the corporation, the broader the range of extras. Yet many large companies grant only a few of the most common ones, such as company cars, reserved parking spaces, medical exams and club memberships. Smaller companies, on the other hand, are sometimes most lavish; of nine companies in the AMA survey that granted a top executive the use of company-owned or leased housing, seven had assets of less than $200 million, and one company with sales under $25 million provided its CEO with a staff of domestic servants.

The decision as to which extras a CEO and his colleagues will receive is in most cases made by the CEO himself, since he knows how he wants those favors distributed. He has four principal kinds of assorted extras to choose from.

• *Privileges.* Better appointed and located office; reserved parking space; executive (or private) washroom; executive dining room; early retirement option.

- *Services.* Free medical examinations; comprehensive medical coverage; club memberships; business credit card; financial counseling; legal counseling; tax assistance; free or low-cost loans; chauffeur for business and-/or personal use; moving and relocation costs; hotel and travel reservations; tickets for theatre and sports events.
- *Equipment.* Company car for business and/or personal use; company plane for business and/or personal use; company yacht or boat for business and/or personal use; hotel suite; rent-free house or apartment; resort facilities.
- *Expense allowances.* Vacation allowances; vacation expenses; wife's travel expenses; home entertainment allowance; expense accounts; educational grants for children; paid attendance at business and professional meetings; barber and beauty shop expenses; nursing home care.

No corporation has yet disclosed what a typical assortment of extras for one executive might add up to in one year. Undoubtedly the total would be large indeed. Consider that a company car with a chauffeur could represent a tax-free bonus of $15,000 a year; that legal counseling might be worth $500 a year and financial counseling another $3,000; that club memberships could amount to $8,000 a year; that allowances for vacations and a wife's travel expenses might add another $8,000.

Still other valuable extras might include an interest-free loan worth $7,500, and the use of the company's executive dining room, its aircraft and its apartment facilities could be worth $9,000 or more a year. One consultant has estimated that a collection of such perks given to an executive at the $200,000 salary level would be equivalent to $35,500 to $55,-500 in additional salary. The single benefit of complete medical coverage, including nursing care, might easily involve more money than all the other extras put together.

A director who reviews the size and range of the extras now granted management may be pardoned for experiencing a few sharp twinges of envy, considering the meager favors directors have been receiving.

What's a Director Worth?

Corporate directors are the only denizens of the corporate world who are legally permitted to set their own rewards. Yet most of them have never done so; they have allowed management to decide the amount of their annual retainers and meeting fees as part of the compensation package proposed for the board's rubberstamp approval.

Even where a compensation committee exists it rarely tackles this compensation problem, primarily because it is still impossible to say what a director may be worth. It can be argued that directors who attend ten or twelve meetings a year, eat heavy lunches and casually accept management's decisions and proposals are not even worth the $20 gold pieces that were once passed out at board meetings. On the other hand, if directors really did the work of keeping fully informed about their corporations, really set their policies, monitored their managements and wrestled with their problems, then their present rewards might seem far too modest.

As it is, the fees and retainers awarded directors now cover an enormous range.* Surveys have shown that, roughly speaking, directors of corporations with more than $500 million in assets receive from $200 to $2,500 for each of the meetings (from four to fourteen) they attend annually. Additional compensation for work on board committees may add $25,000 or more to the total. There is no predictable pattern to such payments beyond the fact that the larger corporations usually pay more than the smaller ones. In 1975 the median figure for the biggest corporations (over $1 billion in assets) was $11,500 per director.

But such statistical generalization can be misleading. In 1975 a large office equipment manufacturer paid its directors retainers of $5,000 plus $350 per meeting, while a competitor with one-third the assets paid no meeting fee at all but to some directors awarded a retainer of $30,000 for a minimum of thirty days work on board business. Similarly, a small motor vehicle maker paid some directors $24,000 a year (half in fees, half in retainer), which was about twice what the three biggest auto companies gave their board members for regular board service.

A considerable number of corporations (one in five manufacturing companies) pay some directors twice, as board members and as employees. Fees per meeting for the inside directors run from $20 to $600; retainers range from $2,000 to $12,000 a year. Paid inside directors are prevalent among transportation, mining, insurance and public utility companies.

The brightest spot in directors' compensation is the additional money paid to committee chairmen, particularly those

*Figures cited here are mostly from surveys by the Conference Board and the American Management Association.

heading the executive and finance committees. About one corporation in ten pays committee chairmen extra, with retainers generally ranging from $500 to $25,000 (and occasionally much higher). At least two large corporations in 1975 paid their executive committee chairmen $75,000, and a third awarded its finance committee chairman $90,000. Chairmen of other committees receive much less; audit and compensation committee chairmen get $250 to $15,000 for their work.

Extra rewards are also given to directors who have special status inside or outside the company. These include retired officers and consultants and in some cases (notably public utility companies) the board chairman, who may be an outside director. In five such cases in 1975 the annual retainers ranged from $12,000 to $34,000.

Directors, however, are forgotten men when it comes to special benefits and perks. While nearly all corporations reimburse them for travel expenses to attend meetings, only one in six pays for travel insurance. An AMA survey of 667 companies in 1975 showed that less than 3 percent of the corporations provided directors with a car and/or a chauffeur or paid their wives' travel expenses; only one company in twelve furnished company planes for business trips; and only about one company in a hundred provided directors with legal or financial counsel or the use of company-owned resort facilities and hotel suites.

A similarly bleak view of directors' benefits was revealed by a Conference Board survey in 1975. Of nearly 1,000 companies, only eleven gave directors discounts on their products, only five offered stock options, only two provided pensions, only one assigned a car and only one paid for club memberships.

The only benefit now enjoyed by nearly all directors is insurance against liabilities and expenses resulting from legal action. Practically every corporation now indemnifies its directors against personal loss in such cases, and three out of four companies carry "directors' and officers' liability insurance" to reimburse individuals for liabilities and expenses not indemnified by the company. Coverage here ranged between $1 million and $50 million in 1975, but nearly half the companies offered $5 million or less.

7

Monitoring Management

The Board's Watchdog: The Audit Committee

A director who is appointed to the audit committee of a large corporation today has been handed the unpopular, delicate and complex job of keeping tabs on management. As a member of a small subcommittee of the full board he will be charged with keeping a sharp eye on both management and the outside auditors for the protection of the directors as well as the stockholders.

The need for such protection has become increasingly acute as management has taken over most of the responsibilities that belong to the board according to state laws. That need, however, was universally ignored until the late 1930s, when the McKesson & Robbins case, involving fraudulent accounting practices, moved the SEC to recommend that audit committees be made a standard part of publicly held corporations. Even the New York Stock Exchange suggested that outside auditors be selected by a board committee that excluded corporate officers.

These recommendations lay dormant for more than thirty years because directors continued to believe that management would be frank with them. But by 1970 the Penn Central fiasco and the financial high-jinks of merger-happy managements had jolted many directors, and in 1972 the SEC again urged corporations to set up audit committees. This time both the New York Stock Exchange and the American Institute of CPAs endorsed the idea. Following the Watergate exposures of illegal political payments and overseas bribery by large corporations, audit committees multiplied swiftly.

As the New York Stock Exchange pointed out in 1973, an audit committee "no longer represents a corporate luxury but has become a necessity." By 1976 nearly 90 percent of the 1,520 companies listed on the New York Stock Exchange had audit committees or were about to establish them. And in January 1977 the Exchange's directors finally adopted a rule that makes audit committees mandatory by June 30, 1978, for companies listed on that exchange. (Canada made them mandatory in 1971.)

An effective audit committee is expected to question both management and outside auditors on a very broad list of complex subjects. These range from compensating balances, doubtful receivables, unasserted claims and inventory methods to capitalization policies, company loans, intangible assets and tax problems. One "working guide" for audit committees published by Price, Waterhouse & Co. includes forty-two different "suggested topics to be discussed during meetings with independent accountants, financial management representatives, internal auditors and others."

As the audit committee's prime job is to make sure that the full board gets no surprises in the financial data management submits to it, obviously, at least one member of the committee has to be astute financially. The committee should schedule a minimum of three meetings a year, one toward the end of the year to outline the scope of the audit, the second when the year-end figures are ready for review, and the third when the outside auditor's "management letter," with its questions and recommendations, has been reviewed and action recommended.

On the basis of its findings the committee may be asked by the full board to recommend a change in the outside auditors. This should be done whenever the board feels that the auditors are taking orders from management. (The accounting partner handling the work should at least be rotated every three to five years.) Because their allegiance is primarily to management, which has hired them, outside auditors usually report financial figures in the manner management wants them reported: to make management look good. This often produces distorted or fraudulent reports—for which the directors are ultimately responsible.

While outside auditors may say, "If we can't trust management we have to resign," the fact remains that some auditors go right on signing statements that support questionable or misleading information supplied by management. There are auditors who believe that some illegal acts on the part of management—such as a billion-dollar corporation's setting up a $10 million "slush fund" for secret payments—are not "material" enough to be reported.

One of the most valuable functions of the audit committee is to recommend and follow through on seeing that the internal audit department is upgraded and strengthened. Shrewd collusion between management and its internal auditors can evade the best controls; thus both the audit committee and the outside auditors ought to maintain a healthy skepticism toward all reports and figures received from management.

There is still argument among directors over whether management should be represented on the audit committee. Those who favor it claim that in this way the committee can obtain a fuller picture of operations and problems and that a corporate officer's being on the committee can minimize the friction that can occur between management, the outside auditors and the committee. Nevertheless, the SEC and most directors now seem convinced that only outside directors should serve on audit committees.

There is, however, no accepted definition of an outside director, as the New York Stock Exchange found in working out its new mandatory audit committee policy. After months of analyzing the suggestions and objections it solicited from the CEOs of listed companies, the Exchange eliminated from its final draft all references to outside directors and "independent directors." Its policy states that an audit committee shall be "comprised solely of directors independent of management and free from any relationship that, in the opinion of its Board of Directors, would interfere with the exercise of independent judgment as a committee member."

This policy obviously leaves a board a lot of leeway even within the guidelines—and loopholes—provided by the Exchange to assist directors "to observe the spirit of the Policy." Thus while officers (and their close relatives) and employees of the company would not be qualified to serve on the audit committee of a listed company, a former officer on pension might, as could also lawyers, consultants and other professional advisors who directly served and were paid by the board—but not if they or their firms regularly served management and the relationship was "material" to the company, their firms or themselves. That is, a highly paid lawyer or executive might qualify if the board decided that what he received for his services to management was not materially significant to him.

No such fine distinctions need be made about an inside director. He cannot be expected to remain objective about his corporation's financial posture and condition because his own career in the company may be critically affected by what the audit committee discovers. And the presence of one dominant CEO or financial officer can quickly impair the committee's credibility.

The "sensitive" areas, those that call for close inspection by the committee, should be discussed with the outside auditors before and after every audit. Several such areas are: changes in operations or debt, environmental regulations, ERISA, tax positions, internal auditing controls, inventories, receivables, foreign exchange, aging of accounts, and—most important—accounting methods.

Some of the knottiest problems for the committee are produced by the profusion and confusion of accounting techniques. For years the accounting profession has failed to come up with new and better accounting principles. By 1976 three Financial Accounting Standards Boards had collapsed in waves of heated controversy over such principles, and the fourth FASB effort had set up one accounting rule, Standard No. 8, that infuriated the managements of many multinational corporations.

The FASB-8 rule required corporations to translate their foreign-denominated assets and liabilities into dollars to reflect gains or losses in each quarterly report. This meant that management could no longer use a chaotic variety of methods to postpone or hide the ups and downs in income caused by fluctuations in foreign currencies. Under the new rule, some quarterly reports of earnings gyrated so wildly that several major multinational corporations found their financial statements swimming in red ink.

More managements today seem inclined to bring "sensitive" matters to the audit committee and even to the full board. This is sometimes done at the urging of the outside auditor, who is himself usually reluctant to go directly to the committee. And committee members, to avoid embarrassing the CEO, may prefer to discuss such matters with him privately and then meet with the outside auditor to get his side of the story.

Another sticky problem for the audit committee is the conflict between the outside auditors and the corporation's outside counsel. While accountants back the SEC mandate for full disclosure, the lawyers hold to the tradition of protecting a confidential relationship with their clients. The auditors can't be sure that management has reported to them all the potential liabilities (known as "unasserted claims") that could affect the corporation's financial status. Such liabilities include illegal campaign gifts, infringement on patents or another company's property, and unfulfillable long-term contracts; an outside counsel who does not regard these as actual liabilities may refuse to report them to the auditors, claiming he has to protect such confidential information from disclosure or his client would refuse to discuss such important matters with him.

Conflicts of interest among management personnel and other employees may be a problem for the committee, and these may be carefully hidden. One director has recommended using questionnaires to ferret them out, even though it sounds naive to expect an employee to tattle on himself.

The audit committee will have to weigh prudently the costs of making an in-depth investigation of "sensitive" areas. Such costs may run from $25,000 to more than $1 million and could become prohibitive if undertaken regularly. Realizing this, even the SEC recommends that the committee's investigations be made on a cyclical basis, perhaps every three or four years.

Finally, there is the possibility that the audit committee will uncover something that some on the committee will not vote to investigate. Then a conscientious director may adopt what the SEC calls the "self-help remedy" and personally disclose the facts to outside authorities.

The Weakest Link: Appraising Management

Directors have written and talked about their duties and responsibilities, but they have all but ignored their principal task, that of monitoring and evaluating top management as carefully as management itself tries to score its subordinates. And the most critically important aspect of that task— removing an incompetent CEO—is never discussed, even after firing has taken place.

Any experienced director knows why directors are reluctant to face these two major responsibilities. Inside directors don't dare to criticize the CEO because their careers in the corporation are based on their compatibility with the boss; as long as an inside director is satisfied with the money, opportunities and recognition he receives, he does not presume to judge his benefactor.

The posture of the outside director is different, but he is equally (and often more) inhibited from passing judgment;

he is nearly always a loyal friend of the CEO belonging to the same clubs, holding the same views and moving in the same social strata. And he is often himself a CEO who feels an obligation to protect another member of this exclusive fraternity who is probably a director on his own board. Or the outside director may be at the mercy of a dominant stockholder or a board chairman who is not the CEO. If the director sides with the CEO, the top man can find ways of easing him off the board as a disloyal or embarrassing troublemaker.

All this ingrown compatibility normally produces intense reactions when critics question the way in which the corporation is being run. Yet almost all outside directors who have thought seriously about their responsibilities are frustrated and disillusioned by the impotence of their positions. They would like to be more effective—indeed, it is widespread frustration, more than the fear of liability suits, that is most responsible for the decline in the number of persons willing to accept directorships.

At the same time the growing reluctance of those qualified to serve on boards enables a strong CEO to increase his protection against serious, careful appraisal. He can persuade the board to revert to the old system of "inside" boards (directorships limited to officers and executives subservient to the CEO), or he can select more directors from the ranks of lawyers, consultants and investment bankers who can be counted on to support the CEO because they usually find their directorships profitable.

Because of all the loyalties, pressures, inhibitions and self-interests it is not surprising that the task of appraising management has been called the weakest link in the entire corporate structure. Far more surprising is the fact that so little effort has been made to find a practical means of monitoring the CEO. Nearly all who have recognized its essential importance have glossed over the problem of *how* to measure and score management. A direct, specific approach to this task is thought to be an unseemly infringement of the CEO's authority that would deeply offend his ego and make him an adversary of the board. And these apprehensions are probably correct for most big corporations today; they are clear symptoms of the respectful attitudes that the management takeover has induced in directors.

The job of appraising management is usually couched in broad generalizations of what the board "should" do. Some say the board should "review" the CEO's policies, procedures, performance and staffing; others call for "evaluating" the corporation's strategies, objectives and the "quality of its management." Some recommend that board members meet privately with the CEO to discuss "sensitive" points concerning his performance, his ability to set goals and to manage.

Few directors have proposed specific ways of measuring the CEO's performance. They agree generally that the most logical approach is to establish performance standards for the job after conferring with the CEO on the areas most significant for that company. Standards would assess corporate strategies, tactics, short-term and long-term objectives and critical areas that might determine the corporation's success.

Even with a very cooperative CEO to work with, setting up a specific table of performance standards is likely to be a touchy, complex and unpleasant job. Nevertheless the idea is sound, and there are ways of accomplishing it without undertaking a microscopic statistical and psychological analysis of the CEO.

8

What's the Prescription?

1. Give the Board Its Own Staff?

Giving the board of directors its own staff sounds like the most practical and rational means of reducing the ignorance of directors about their corporations. It would need only the vote of the directors to establish staff and facilities for regularly gathering information concerning the corporation and reporting its findings directly to the board.

This is not likely to happen. Directors with the courage to propose such an innovation are almost nonexistent. Chief executives who would agree to it are even rarer. Any director who insists that the board have its own staff can expect martyrdom.

Witness the fate of Arthur J. Goldberg, former Associate Justice of the Supreme Court, former Ambassador to the United Nations and former director of Trans World Airlines. On October 18, 1972, after sixteen months as a TWA director, he shook up the corporate world by announcing his resignation from that board. Even more remarkably, he spelled out the reason why: "My reason for resigning is that under the company's existing procedures I do not find it possible to fulfill my legal and public obligations as a member of the Board." What he had insisted on, he explained, was that the outside directors should meet independently and hire a staff of technical specialists to help them judge the policies recommended by management.

The "existing procedures" he objected to are the common practice of large corporate boards: outside directors are expected to get all their information about the company from top management and are rarely permitted to question corporate officers privately (i.e., in the absence of the chief executive). Under these unwritten rules, a chief executive can, by carefully editing and filtering the data he presents to the board, influence the board's decisions according to his views. Often those views and his judgment have misled directors, causing them to approve acquisitions and mergers, for example, that produced disastrous losses for the corporation.

Management's prerogative to control and color the information given to the board is heavily protected. A chief executive can rely absolutely on the support of inside directors who are his subordinate officers, and he can assume that the outside directors he has personally chosen and befriended will not seriously question his presentations to the board.

Because Arthur Goldberg violated this tradition, TWA's eleven other outside directors and the five inside officer-directors stood unanimously behind management and bid him an empty farewell: "While the other members of the T.W.A. Board do not share the views advanced by Mr. Goldberg for his resignation, they greatly regret the resignation from the T.W.A. Board of one who has distinguished himself in so many areas of public service. He has had an outstanding career and will be missed from the Board's deliberations."

The Goldberg proclamation was a direct hit on management's most sensitive nerve. For he had tried, without success, to persuade the board to hire technical specialists to help the board review management's decisions. He had raised the familiar, crucial question, What are the responsibilities and prerogatives of the board and of management?

The question is a red flag to every chief executive of a large corporation who believes he holds the authority to plan and run his organization as *he* determines. Goldberg's dictum was therefore ill-conceived and premature; it cannot be considered seriously until the roles of management and the board are separated and clarified. Thus the idea of giving the board its own staff has to be counted as an idea whose time has not yet come.

2. Make the Corporate Secretary and His Staff Responsible Only to the Board?

From the discussion of Prescription number 1 it's clear that it's unrealistic at this point to expect the board to acquire its own staff. However, a great deal can be achieved by making use of a staff that already exists in most large public corporations. This is the staff that, usually under the supervision of the corporate secretary, prepares material about the company for presentation to the board by the chief executive. Basically these are reports on operations, finances, marketing, R&D and planning that are provided by department heads and officers.

Under present procedures such material is normally sub-

mitted to the chief executive and his key associates for review, and they go over it with a sharp eye for anything that
might reflect unfavorably on management. These references
are edited out or revised so that the directors will not become
unduly alarmed or critical. Rarely is the board given a fully
objective report on discouraging or unfavorable developments.

Two changes in this procedure would make it extremely
useful to the board: (1) have the corporate secretary submit
the collected reports directly to the board (and, simultaneously, to the chief executive) and (2) assign one or more
directors to monitor the collecting and assembling of information from the various officers and department heads. The
monitoring task is necessary because executives naturally
tend to doctor to some extent the reports they submit,
thereby minimizing their errors and problems. But this tend-
ency should disappear once they are convinced that the
board wants their unexpurgated reports and will not penalize
them for speaking out.

One of the most valuable by-products for the board of such
a reporting system would be to cut down on the costly management practice of buying elaborate "directors' reports."
Over the years top managements of large corporations have
repeatedly engaged consultants and other specialists in order
to convince the board by their reports that it should approve
acquisitions that management considers promising or "essential." And time and again such acquisitions have turned
out to be disasters that had to be liquidated or sold at tremendous write-offs.

This sequence has been so blatant that some stockholders
have sued directors for failing to protect the assets under
their care. Neither the acquisitions nor the suits would have

taken place, in all probability, had the directors insisted on having the full, unvarnished, unedited story directly from the corporate secretary and his staff.

3. Separate the CEO from the Board Chairmanship?

The CEO who also assumes the post of board chairman is the most obvious exponent of the management takeover. The practice has become a standard feature of nearly all large corporations to the extent that it is difficult to find a major company where the top executive is not also the board chairman in effect if not in title.

This combining of responsibilities represents a bold assumption of authority. By becoming board chairman, the CEO has it both ways: not only does he generally set the policies and strategies of the corporation, he also counts himself among those qualified to approve those policies and strategies and to judge his own performance in carrying them out.

Arguments in favor of the CEO's acquiring the additional responsibilities of chairman are not convincing. One says that the CEO as chairman will see to it that the board considers and acts on every important problem—but the CEO's self-interest in concealing certain problems makes this argument suspect. A more reasonable argument says that the CEO knows more about the corporation than any of the directors—but this does not justify his being the one who decides how the board shall go about its business of reviewing and judging the intelligence he can provide. A third argument holds that the CEO as board chairman can prevent the development of what is euphemistically called "an adversary relationship" between board and management—unfortunately, he can also prevent the board from assuming its responsibilities as an objective critic of management.

There are more cogent arguments in favor of separating the CEO from the board chairmanship. If this is done, the board has a better chance of achieving the independence it needs to function as monitor and judge of management. It can select candidates for the board who are not beholden to the CEO; it can set its own standards for compensating the CEO and his staff; it will be less inhibited in appraising—or firing—the CEO if he is seen as a subordinate of the board.

Few corporations have attempted this radical surgery to cure the impotence of the board. One pioneer is Texas Instruments, Inc., which restructured its board to provide its chairman with the time "to study, to think quietly about, and to comprehend the importance" of the corporation's internal and external environments and its changing opportunities. The chairman "is usually the chief corporate officer, but only by virtue of his responsibilities [for policies and performance] as chairman of the board." And the president, as the CEO responsible for "the detailed management of the corporation," reports to the entire board, not to the chairman.

Another champion of the separation of powers is Courtney C. Brown, dean emeritus of Columbia's Graduate School of Business. In his book *Putting the Corporate Board to Work,* Brown calls for "a partial shift of authority, an identification and division of functions between management and the board, and a progressive separation of management from board personnel." He also recommends that board committees take over many of the CEO's tasks of setting objectives, strategies and policies and dealing with the corporation's various publics.

Management can be counted on to oppose strenuously the idea of keeping the CEO from the board chairmanship. Thus directors may frequently have to become adversaries of their CEOs—or at least skeptical, good-natured critics. But unless they do, there can be no real reversal of the management takeover.

4. Appoint Public Directors Who Will Hold Corporations Accountable?

The appointment of directors who will hold corporations accountable to the public has often been proposed by those who believe that the public must have a direct voice in corporate policies, strategies and decisions. The assumption is that independent, publicly appointed directors can best represent those whose interests are not now diligently protected by directors or management (i.e., stockholders, employees, consumers and the general public).

So far this assumption remains untested. The closest we have come to having public directors are the federal officials appointed to represent the interests of the government on the boards of some agencies and joint ventures. The controller of the currency, for example, is one of three directors of the Federal Deposit Insurance Corporation.

Obviously the major corporations would not welcome public directors. A board member who would investigate and report publicly on how well the corporation is discharging its responsibilities to its various publics could embarrass the other directors and impair management's authority.

However, it is the means of providing public directors that inevitably raises the thorniest questions. Some specific answers have come from Robert Townsend, former board chairman of Avis Rent A Car Corp., who has proposed that every corporation with over $1 billion in assets provide a $1 million annual budget to finance the salary of a public director ($50,000 a year was suggested) and the costs of hiring scientists, engineers, lawyers and accountants to answer the questions the other directors weren't asking. The public director would have an office in the company's headquarters, he or a member of his staff would have access to all meetings, offices and files in the company and he would report to the press at least twice a year on how the company handled issues of public interest. Public directors would be assigned to corporations by lot and be rotated every four years.

Townsend recognized the critical point: who would select the public directors? He suggested an ad hoc committee of congressmen who had at least been vice presidents in non-family businesses and who would require candidates to meet these criteria: ten or more years experience in line and staff jobs in a big corporation; sufficient wealth and disinterest in corporate power to be incorruptible; reasonable energy and intelligence.

Townsend spotted many of the pitfalls in his own plan. Management would try to take over the selection of public directors and, failing that, would try to bury them in futile assignments and computer printouts, would put ringers on their staffs and would shift important business matters from standing board committees to anonymous committees. But Townsend believed that an experienced public director could counter these traps and evasions by surreptitiously securing information from managers who were "cool to what management is doing or failing to do." According to Townsend, "If implemented properly, a public director could be the vehicle to make a real dent into corporate accountability." This "if" leaves a lot of details to be specified.

It is these specifics that the lawyer Christopher D. Stone supplies in his book, *Where the Law Ends.* * Stone points out that merely adding public directors to corporate boards won't work because the concept of "public interest" is too vague to guide directors' decisions and because serious social issues involving the corporation are rarely brought to the board before the harm has been done. Like Townsend, he knows that with public directors on a board, management would find ways to shift problems to a clubby committee so that few of them would reach the board as a whole.

However, Stone argues that for these very reasons it is necessary to restructure the board, and he cites six ways of doing it. Even with these changes, he believes, major problems of corporate behavior will not be countered. Therefore he prescribes the appointment, by courts or government agencies, of two different kinds of public directors.

A General Public Director, nominated by the SEC or a Federal Corporation Commission, would have offices in the company quarters and a fulltime staff and would function as a superego in preventing or dealing with the possible consequences of corporate acts. He would watch for violations of legal restrictions, act as liaison to public agencies, monitor the company's information system, be a hot line to the board for managers on lower levels, monitor the directors' adherence to their functions and act as a director for the entire corporation's interest.

A Special Public Director would handle two kinds of situations: where a company has shown continued delin-

*Christopher D. Stone, *Where the Law Ends* (New York, Harper & Row, 1975)

quent behavior that legal mechanisms won't cope with and where there is a generic industry problem such as the asbestos poisoning of workers. He would be professionally expert in such problems and the relevant laws, keep public authorities informed of conditions in the company and recommend changes in organization and operating standards.

Both of these public directors would have the power to inspect company books and records, request surveys, sit on all committees and prevent the firing of any employee cooperating with them (and have a voice in rewarding them). The public directors could bring suit against anyone in the company who obstructed their functions.

Both Townsend's and Stone's proposals leave questions unanswered. What legal or constitutional basis is needed to introduce a public agent permanently into the private affairs of a corporation? Who would establish the criteria for selecting public directors? (Would court judges or government agencies or former businessmen in Congress be qualified to screen and choose directors capable of appraising the complex issues involved in corporate behavior?) How much could a public director report to outsiders about a corporation's troubles without hampering the efforts of management and the other directors to solve them?

5. Recapture the Proxy System?

Granted that "stockholder democracy" is an idle fiction and that it is naive to expect that management's control through the proxy system can be curbed directly by stockholders acting together; nevertheless the situation is not as unchangeable as some directors—and practically all chief executives

—would argue. As long as the law holds that stockholders have the right to vote their shares in electing directors, stockholders have the right to choose.

And it is the directors who have the authority to see that stockholders in fact have that right. They can begin by recapturing the proxy system from management, and then they can take several other steps. Specifically, the following actions appear feasible:

1. Remove the proxy system from the chief executive's control and give it to a committee of three outside directors.

2. Have this committee select all candidates for directorships.

3. Have the proxy ballot include a slate of more candidates for the board than are to be elected (e.g., shareholders might be given a choice of electing three out of five).

4. Require that each candidate on the ballot be fully described—career, experience, interests and personal background—with a photograph and a statement from each as to why he would accept the responsibilities of board membership.

5. Send out all proxies clearly marked, "solicited on behalf of the directors."

6. Make public the voting results, including the names and numbers of votes cast by "beneficial owners" and the institutional holdings.

If these measures were introduced, the proxy system would function somewhat as it does in a small, privately held company. The board would secure its authority over management as owner-manager-directors have always done; voters would select candidates whose credentials were visible; and

large stockholders would identify their convictions and preferences with respect to the corporation.

6. A Scorecard for Rating Management*

The final "prescription in this book is, in the author's opinion, the most promising because it offers outside directors
practical means of doing their fundamental job: rating management.

The scorecard idea, developed after years of frustration in
trying to assess management's performance, is still in an
experimental stage. The formula presented here will of
course have to be adapted to each individual company, for
the weighting of factors will vary from board to board and
not all the factors will necessarily be scored in some companies.

The scorecard is not a clinical analysis. It is more like a
simple test of blood pressure that will indicate generally
whether the CEO is on a survival course or is headed for deep
trouble. If the rating is done every three months or so, it can
be far more useful than the annual physical checkup that has
become a fairly standard requirement for top executives.

The scorecard has two parts, one for general factors and
the other for personal factors. This helps directors to see the
CEO from two sides. His performance as shown by financial
and operating results must be interpreted in the light of his
personal behavior inside and outside the company that has
an effect on the company and its various publics. He may, for

*Many of the elements described here first appeared in an article, "A Score Card
for Rating Management" by Edward McSweeney in the June 8, 1974, issue of
Business Week.

example, be turning in a striking performance in financial growth while neglecting the development of local goodwill (which in time could have unfortunate consequences).

The process of scoring the CEO should be kept simple and preferably nonstatistical. Operating and financial figures can be used to rate some of the items by comparing them with those of competitive companies. Most of the items, however, will be rated by the directors' judgments based on their individual business know-how. Directors may do this by asking themselves pertinent questions and recording their answers in the approximate terms, "good," "fair" and "poor."

Probably no two directors would use this scorecard in the same way in assessing a CEO and his performance; each will apply his own subjective judgment. But if eight or ten or twelve outside directors pool the results of their ratings, the net judgment is likely to be accurate overall, regardless of individual variations.

Here is how the factors might be listed:

GENERAL SCORECARD

1. Return on stockholders' equity (compare with competitors').
2. Return on sales (compare with competitors').
3. Percentage of industry by segments.
4. Management of stockholders' assets.

Management usually keeps this activity pretty well concealed, but directors should be able to secure the information without too much trouble. How the treasurer, controller or financial vice president handles the corporation's money may be very significant (in one case in which the assets had been dissipated it took considerable searching to discover this).

5. Development of sound organization.

A company is no better than its organization structure, and as it grows the structure needs to be revised constantly. The quality of the CEO's staff is extremely important. The recent trend toward establishing two or three top executives as an "office of the president" recognizes that the complexity of the top job can become too great for one man to handle. Some corporate leaders (like the late Alfred P. Sloan of General Motors) haven't accepted this and continue to believe in one-man leadership. But there are two functions in running a business: the internal task of operations and the external tasks of building the company image and handling community and industry relations. The civic obligations may become so demanding that the CEO simply can't run the business and do all the other things he's expected to do.

6. Development of the corporate image.

This is part of the organization problem. A director can often tell how good or how bad the image is by the company's ease of access to the financial community. The old definition of a successful organization as "the shadow of one man" (exemplified by Sloan and General Motors) ignores the fact that the image will fall as the big man's shadow falls unless the corporation is organized as well as GM's has been. If a director can spot questionable qualities in the CEO, it's likely that others below him in the organization have weaknesses, too—and a slick public relations campaign cannot hide them for long.

7. Development of successors.

This is of great importance. A very strong CEO almost

never wants a very strong No. 2 man—and he rarely believes that he's not going to live forever. That's why so
many companies have to go outside to find replacements
for the top man. This may work out, but the risk will
always be there: the weak No. 2 man won't be building up
strong successors either. The best policy is to make every
promotion dependent on the development of a strong and
qualified successor.

8. Development of proprietary products.
This is the major asset on many balance sheets. It is often
a trade name (like Anacin) that has tremendous hidden
value because it has taken a lot of time and money to
establish it in the market. How a CEO develops or retains
such an asset can be a significant factor in his performance.

9. Development of growth potential.
What the financial community looks for is a 10 percent
increase annually in sales and earnings over a period of
years. It is important to be able to trace the sources of
profits and losses exactly and continuously and then see
that the CEO acts to control them.

10. Development of organization morale.
Directors can be rather easily fooled by pleasant, cheerful-
sounding executives and managers who surround the
CEO. Poor morale is not easily assessed, but it is inevitably
the reflection of poor management. However, the CEO is
not likely to concede this, and he may try to influence the
board with informal talks and plant visits. Directors can
get a much better picture of morale from employee attitude surveys if these are conducted so as to protect absolutely the identities of those answering the questionnaires.

11. Acquisitions and divestments.
The success achieved in these ventures is not hard to detect

after the fact. The difficult thing is to assess the chances of success beforehand, on the basis of what the CEO, the lawyers and the consultants tell the board. The CEO's urge to conglomerate may be simply his urge to look like a big operator. While he may do a superb job in acquiring a company, he may mess things up badly in spinning off a subsidiary.

12. Application of Research & Development.

The CEO may or may not have a feel for this, but the board ought to know what's going on in the scientific and technological worlds, and it should have regular expert rundowns on new developments. CEOs who are biased toward finance, engineering or marketing are especially blind to the potential commercial fallout of a new product or process reported by a laboratory.

13. International operations.

The lure of becoming a multinational corporation is usually irresistible to an overoptimistic CEO. Directors had better get themselves well briefed on the complications involved in such a move before they let themselves be persuaded to go along. If the CEO minimizes the currency risks and the tricky management problems of overseas operations, he deserves a "poor" rating by the board.

14. Why is the company in business?

This is an important question that is not likely to be raised at all by the CEO or by the directors. To assess the company's reasons for being in business involves looking hard into its history, considering how it reached its present state and then asking a lot of pertinent questions. Does the company serve a real need? Are its products what people should have? Has its success been built on deception and high-powered advertising? Is the company aiming at the wrong markets? A CEO's answers to these questions can reveal a good deal about his leadership capacities.

PERSONAL SCORECARD

1. Corporate citizenship.

A CEO may be carried away by some current idea of corporate responsibility or by his desire for public recognition. What does he give back to the community? Does he make a reasonable contribution of time and effort to community and government, or does he overdo it?

2. Interlocking directorships.

The urge of CEOs to sit on a lot of corporate and other boards has abated drastically, but too many still sit on more boards than they can reasonably contribute to. Directors should also make sure that in the CEO's other directorates he is not risking conflicts of interests.

3. Outside business activities.

If the CEO has many outside interests, what percentage of his time should he give to the company that is paying him $100,000 or more? How much do his outside interests contribute to the company and how much to the CEO personally?

4. Health.

A periodic medical report on the CEO's physical condition should be available to the directors. Is he trying to handle everything himself to the point of exhaustion? Does he watch his physical condition closely or does he ignore it? Is there any question about his use of alcohol?

5. Builder of human resources.

The CEO has to be scored as a manager of people as well as of things. Is he trying seriously to develop his subordinates as their coach, teacher and counselor? Or is he aloof, expecting others to perform this task? Does he keep an eye on promising young managers and let them know he is watching them?

6. Selection of officers.

Because directors now commonly leave the selection and appointment of top officers to the CEO, his choices and methods deserve close inspection. Does he simply introduce his candidates at luncheons, dinners or other meetings and expect the board to approve them? Does he provide data on their backgrounds and qualifications, or does he emphasize their social status, club memberships and personal connections? Has he made deals with any of them privately, involving compensation, fringe benefits and perquisites?

7. Decisiveness.

The CEO rarely brings his toughest management problems to the board, and since inside directors are discreet outside directors often don't know how he meets and solves those problems. Does he depend on committees? Does he postpone action on a problem that might go away? Does he make major decisions arbitrarily without consulting the board? Can he live with his decisions, or does he develop tensions and anxiety when things turn out poorly?

8. Trading in company stock.

The board must watch closely lest the CEO (and members of the board) violate SEC restrictions on the use of corporate information by insiders for personal profit. A CEO who trades heavily though legally in his company holdings can be scored as a speculator rather than a manager.

Other factors will have to be added to the scorecards to cover special situations and personalities. But before any scoring can be applied the directors themselves will have to pass their test: Are they ready to assume the responsibility of evaluating the CEO's performance—and removing him if he doesn't measure up?

9

What's Ahead?

Once Again, Federal Chartering Comes Alive

In the post-Watergate era of the 1970s big public corporations were charged with many failings—fraudulent management, impotent directors, indifference to stockholders' and public interests, deceptive accounting and advertising practices, environmental pollution. And inevitably a 200-year-old demand was heard once again: corporations should be chartered and monitored by federal law, not by the states whose weak and poorly enforced laws have left great corporate powers unchecked and unaccountable. As all directors should know, federal chartering could make them far more responsible and liable than they have ever been.

The idea of federal chartering was familiar to the Founding Fathers, who in 1781 considered including it in the Constitution but never voted on it. Madison urged it, but Jefferson feared it would lead to monopolies that could overpower the federal government. And early in the nineteenth century the states got into the competitive business of offering the enterpriser quick and easy incorporation.

The ominous power of the trusts in the 1880s revived the issue, and over the next fifty years federal chartering repeatedly gained powerful support. Among its champions were William Jennings Bryan, Mark Hanna, presidents Theodore Roosevelt, Taft and Wilson, the Democratic and Republican platforms, the *Wall Street Journal,* the NAM and John D. Rockefeller.

Each time, however, an alternative remedy for corporate misbehavior was found as politicians decided in favor of the broader controls of antitrust laws and the regulations of the ICC, the FTC and finally the SEC. Between 1903 and 1932, twenty-eight bills on the chartering or licensing of corporations were introduced in Congress, but all died, as did the charterlike effects of the National Recovery Administration during the Great Depression. In 1938 Senators Borah and O'Mahoney pressed hard for their bill on chartering that included six stiff proposals for controlling corporate power and procedures, but it too expired.

In 1976 the pressure for federal chartering had revived so strongly that both the Senate and the House opened hearings on the subject of unaccountable corporate power under state laws. And Ralph Nader and his Corporate Accountability Research Group published a 592-page report on this issue that they had spent five years preparing.

The basic issue, of course, is still power. Neither the states nor the large corporations relish handing over to federal authorities the social, economic and political power they have achieved under state chartering. Those most strongly opposed are the state of Delaware, which gets 25 percent of its revenues from incorporations, and the countless lawyers who want to keep the income from corporate fees from leaving their states. But there are pros as well as cons, and strong cases have been made for both sides.

Those in favor of federal chartering say that it will (1) stop permissive states from coddling corporations to keep them from shifting their legal headquarters to other states; (2) stop corporations from extorting benefits from states by threatening to move their legal residence; (3) give specific central control over large multinational corporations and diffuse the concentrations of such power; (4) monitor the power corporations have over consumers, the public and the environment; (5) remind corporations that they hold their charters in trust for the benefit of the public; (6) provide penalties for violations.

The case against chartering includes these arguments: the federal government should *not* (1) manipulate the private rights of property; (2) regulate the states; (3) impair the concept of "prior contracts"; (4) cause corporations to move to bases outside the United States to avoid chartering; (5) cause states to suffer losses of tax income; (6) require corporations to obey charters that would include vague and unenforceable standards.

Another great weakness in the chartering concept, which is rarely mentioned by its opponents, is that government agencies that regulate business almost always wind up as the captives of the corporate interests they are supposed to regulate. The history of federal regulation by the ICC, the FTC, the CAB and the FCC is not encouraging in this respect. A federal chartering agency would have to remain independent, but as Ralph Nader has written, "If it is badly organized with weak powers and no citizen access or participation, it will be ineffective."

So the prospects for federal chartering seem not much brighter than they have been in the past. States' righters are a powerful lobby that can be counted on to water down any restrictions on corporate behavior that Congress may eventually consider. Nevertheless some sort of congressional action on the issue seems likely—perhaps by 1980. And the current arguments for federal chartering ought to make directors think harder about their own accountability.

Co-determination: Labor into Management

Co-determination can be defined simply as the socialist's word for letting nonmanagement workers participate in management at the board level. Though no one, as of 1977, was seriously recommending that U.S. corporations import this product, directors of large corporations, with or without foreign affiliations, can expect to hear a lot more about this controversial procedure.

The idea of admitting rank-and-file employees into the board room originated in West Germany following World War II, when the British occupation forces induced the Social Democratic party to adopt it. As a compromise between nationalizing the coal and steel industries in the Rhur valley and using free enterprise methods of management, workers were given equal representation with shareholders on the "supervisory boards" of every steel and coal company.

In 1952 co-determination was adopted for all other major companies in West Germany, but the workers were given only one-third of the seats on the supervisory boards. In July 1976 co-determination with equal participation of labor and capital at the board level was made mandatory (by June

1978) for all West German companies employing more than 2,000 workers—some 600 companies altogether.

The authority of the German supervisory boards is close to that theoretically enjoyed by U.S. directors. They appoint executives, supervise management, approve the annual report, make broad policy decisions and report to the stockholders. They also appoint the management board that is responsible for all day-to-day operations. Shareholders elect half the board members (ten out of twenty in large companies) and the rest are elected by a complex system that represents, proportionately, three groups—wage earners, salaried employees and managers—with a minimum of one from each group.

With local variations, co-determination has spread throughout Europe and Japan. Sweden's law calls for a board of two top managers, two white-collar workers, two blue-collar workers and two foremen, all to be approved by the stockholders. Usually the board has an outside chairman who can cast a tie-breaking vote when needed.

In Holland co-determination is also well established; either the stockholders or the works councils there can veto nominations to the supervisory board. In France the law provides for a two-tier system of boards, but the idea has not as yet been widely adopted.

In England the Labour government has long been pushing for co-determination. However, the trade unions have been resisting the idea, fearing that their bargaining powers would be compromised and that management would play off the workers' councils against the unions. They also dislike the legal responsibilities and liabilities involved and want these limited.

The future of co-determination remains uncertain. Where

the wave of socialism has abated and extreme socialists have been removed from power, as in Sweden and Australia, the demands of labor to participate in management have also abated. Yet whatever happens to this trend away from socialism, workers will undoubtedly continue to fight to hold the gains they have made in getting management to share its decision-making powers with them.

In the United States the first gesture toward co-determination came in 1976 when the United Auto Workers asked for two seats on Chrysler's board of directors. This request faded away during the contract negotiations that year, and the union committee showed little enthusiasm for co-determination. But in presenting the issue to management the UAW was, as one of its vice presidents said, "planting a seed."

For the present, organized labor in the United States seems to share many of the same apprehensions about co-determination as expressed by Britain's trade unionists. However, U.S. management overseas appears likely to be open-minded about it; in 1975, when Chrysler's British subsidiary was in financial trouble, it was management that offered to put unionists on the company's board.

Suggested Reading

Bacon, Jeremy, *Corporate Directorship Practices,* Conference Board and American Society of Corporate Secretaries, Inc., 1975.

Bacon, Jeremy, "Informing Directors and Officers of Legal Do's and Don'ts," *Conference Board Record,* February 1968.

Bacon, Jeremy, "Some Recent Trends in Directorship Practices," *Conference Board Record,* August 1967.

Bacon, Jeremy, and Brown, James K., *Corporate Directorship Practices: Role, Selection and Legal Status of the Board,* Conference Board, Inc., 1975.

Baker, John C., *Directors and Their Functions,* Harvard University Press, 1945.

Berle, A. A., Jr., *The 20th Century Capitalist Revolution,* Harcourt Brace Jovanovich, 1954.

Berle, A. A., Jr., and Means, Gardiner C., *The Modern Corporation and Private Property,* Harcourt Brace Jovanovich, 1968.

"The Board: It's Obsolete Unless Overhauled," *Business Week,* May 22, 1971.

Brandeis, Louis D., *Other People's Money,* Stokes, 1914.

Briloff, Abraham J., *Unaccountable Accounting,* Harper & Row, 1972.

Brown, Courtney C., *Putting the Corporate Board to Work,* Macmillan, 1975.

Brown, Courtney C., and Smith, E. Everett (eds.), *The Director Looks at His Job,* Columbia University Press, 1957.

Bull, George (ed.), *The Director's Handbook,* McGraw-Hill, 1969.

Cabot, Louis W., "Management and the Director," *Conference Board Record,* April 1974.

Capitman, William G., *Panic in the Boardroom,* Anchor Press/Doubleday, 1973.

Chandler, Marvin, "It's Time to Clean Up the Boardroom," *Harvard Business Review,* September-October 1975.

Copeland, Melvin T., and Towl, Andrew R., *The Board of Directors and Business Management,* Division of Research, Graduate School of Business Administration, Harvard University, 1947.

The Corporate Director and the Investing Public, The New York Stock Exchange, November 1965.

Dooley, Peter C., "The Interlocking Directorates," *American Economic Review,* June 1969.

Fawcett, Edmund, "European Companies," *European Community,* July-August 1975.

Galbraith, John Kenneth, *Economics and the Public Purpose,* Houghton Mifflin, 1973.

Grange, William J., and Woodbury, Thomas C., *Corporation Law: Operating Procedures for Officers and Directors,* Ronald Press, 1964.

Hacker, Andrew, *The Corporate Takeover,* Doubleday, 1964.

Hay, Edward N., "A Stronger Role for Corporate Directors," *Men & Management,* 1972.

Heller, Robert, *The Great Executive Dream,* Delacorte Press, 1972.

"How 225 Companies Pay, Use, Protect and Retire Their Directors," *Business Management,* November 1968.

Juran, J. M., and Louden, J. Keith, *The Corporate Director,* American Management Association, 1966.

Koontz, Harold, *The Board of Directors and Effective Management,* McGraw-Hill, 1967.

Koontz, Harold, "Can the Board of Directors Be Effective?" *European Business,* October 1968.

The Labour Party, *The Community and the Company,* Green Paper Report of a Working Group of the Labour Party Industrial Policy Sub-Committee, May 1974.

Larner, Robert J., "Ownership and Control in the 200 Largest Nonfinancial Corporations, 1929 and 1963," *American Economic Review,* September 1966.

Louden, J. Keith, *The Effective Director in Action,* Amacom, 1975.

Lundberg, Ferdinand, *The Rich and the Super-Rich,* Lyle Stuart, 1968.

Mace, Myles L., *The Board of Directors in Small Companies,* Division of Research, Graduate School of Business Administration, Harvard University, 1948.

Mace, Myles L., *Directors: Myth or Reality,* Harvard Business School, 1971.

Mann, Bruce Alan (chairman), *Preventing Directors' Liability Under the Securities Laws, 1976,* Practicing Law Institute, 1976.

Marvin, Michael D., and Fuersich, Janet, "Executive Perquisites," Amacom, 1975.

Mason, Edward S. (ed.), *The Corporation in Modern Society,* Harvard University Press, 1959.

McDougall, W. J., and Fogelberk, G., *Corporate Boards in Canada,* University of Western Ontario, 1968.

McLaughlin, David J., *The Executive Money Map,* McGraw-Hill, 1975.

McSweeney, Edward, "The Director's Dilemma," *Saturday Review,* June 8, 1968.

Mueller, Robert K., *Board Life: Realities of Being a Corporate Director,* Amacom, 1974.

Nader, Ralph, and Green, Mark J., *Corporate Power in America,* Grossman, 1973.

Nader, Ralph, Green, Mark, and Seligman, Joel, *Taming the Giant Corporation,* Norton, 1976.

Ney, Richard, *The Wall Street Gang,* Praeger, 1974.

Sauerhaft, Stan, *The Merger Game,* Thomas Y. Crowell, 1971.

"Selection of Corporate Directors," *Conference Board Record,* May 1965.

The Smallest Company's Board of Directors, Managing the Moderate-Sized Company #3, National Industrial Conference Board, 1969.

Smith, Adam, *The Wealth of Nations,* Modern Library/Random House.

Smith, E. Everett, "Management's Least-Used Asset: The Board of Directors" in *The Dynamics of Management, Management Report #14,* American Management Association, 1958.

Stone, Christopher D., *Where the Law Ends,* Harper & Row, 1975.

Stryker, Perrin, "It's Tricky Work, Being Board Chairman,"
Fortune, May 1960.

Townsend, Robert, "A Modest Proposal: The Public Director," Appendix in Nader and Green, *Corporate Power in
America.*

Vance, Stanley C., *The Corporate Director: A Critical Evalua-
tion,* Dow Jones-Irwin, 1968.

Vance, Stanley C., "See-Saw in the Boardroom," *Conference
Board Report,* January 1974.

"Why Outside Directors Need to Direct," *Business Week,*
July 4, 1970.

Index

141